A PRIMER OF GROUP PSYCHOTHERAPY

Ray Naar, Ph.D.

Clinical Assistant
Professor of Psychiatry
School of Medicine
University of Pittsburgh

HUMAN SCIENCES PRESS, INC.
72 FIFTH AVENUE,
NEW YORK, N.Y. 10011

Printed in the United States of America
23456789   987654321

Library of Congress Cataloging in Publication Data

Naar, Ray.
    A primer of group psychotherapy.

    Bibliography: p. 207
    Includes index.
    1. Group psychotherapy. I. Title. [DNLM: 1. Psycho-
therapy, Group.   WM 430 N111p]
    RC488.N3   616.89'152   LC 81-4244
    ISBN 0-89885-027-4   AACR2

To my parents, the past;
my wife, the present;
my son, the future

CONTENTS

Foreword

This book is a highly personal endeavor. I am a good therapist and a good teacher. I have been engaged in the practice and teaching of psychotherapy for the past fifteen years and I want to share my experiences and knowledge with others. My fantasy is that I am addressing myself to an audience made up of therapists as well as nonprofessionals who want to become acquainted with group psychotherapy in a manner more sophisticated than what popular psychology books offer. I remember, at the beginning of my career, being faced with what seemed to be insurmountable problems that could have been easily avoided had a concerned and knowledgeable teacher shared with me his or her experiences while allowing me to share my concerns. Perhaps, through this book, I can play part of that role with the readers. Although I cannot hear their concerns, I can imagine them because they are probably no different from what mine were.

Some of the details of the anecdotes accompanying the various concepts discussed were altered; the names of the participants were changed. Alterations and changes are intended to protect the anonymity of group members. Throughout the book I have used the terms *clients, patients,* and *group members* interchangeably. This is also true of the terms *group leader* and *group therapist.* I have reserved the appelation *Director* for the group leader conducting a psychodrama.

As in every endeavor, I was, of course, helped by many. My wife, Claudine, not only put up with many lonely hours but constantly encouraged me to complete my task. My son, Walter, greatly helped me with his editorial comments and prodded me along when my motivation was waning. My colleague and friend, Dr. Constance Fisher, Professor of Psychology, Duquesne University, did a magnificent (and merciless) job of editing the manuscript. Ms. Alexis Chantous and Ms. Carole Brown typed the manuscript and put up with my vagaries, pressures, demands, and deadlines.

I wish to thank Carl Rogers whom I have never met but whose writings deeply influenced both my personal and professional ways of being. My gratitude goes to my dear friend, colleague, and trainer in psychodrama, James Sacks, Ph.D.

Above all, I want to thank the people whose lives I have shared, whose tears, joys, laughter, hopes, despairs, dreams, and growth unfold in these pages: the group members.

Chapter 1

A CASE FOR GROUP THERAPY

Group psychotherapy is one of many psychotherapeutic modalities. To advocate its use, one should first present a rationale. Some of the advantages for using group therapy are obvious, materialistic perhaps, but realistic nevertheless. The fees for group therapy are lower than for individual therapy. More people can be seen in the same period of time and it is easier to offer reduction in fees to clients who choose, but cannot afford, psychotherapy from a private practitioner rather than from an institution.

Valid as the above reasons may be, however, they do not justify the use of group therapy in preference to other approaches. Conclusive experimental data comparing various modalities is not yet available, although efforts in that direction are in process.*

*At this time, a major study investigating the outcome of individual, group and family therapy is under way at the Western Psychiatric Institute and Clinic, under the direction of Dr. Stanley Imber.

Until such data become available, however, it is possible to make a case for the preferred use of groups on theoretical grounds by agreeing upon a definition of psychotherapy and then deciding which of the two modalities, individual or group therapy, comes closer to meeting the definition agreed upon.

I will define psychotherapy as the end result of three processes: awareness, closure, and rehearsal of new behaviors. Needless to say, such definition is somewhat arbitrary, and psychotherapy may be defined in many other legitimate and acceptable ways.

AWARENESS

One way of looking at a person's behaviors is in terms of choices. Whatever behavior we enact, we could conceivably engage into the opposite behavior. We can go left or right, stay in bed in the morning or go to work, get a job or acquire more training, etc. Many of our behaviors have become, through habit, almost reflex-like and most of them have survival value. For example, we stop at a red light; we wash, dress, drive, or ride a bus to work; greet our friends; ride elevators; etc. Most of the time these behaviors are quite predictable both by the individual who engages in them and by outside observers. Other types of behaviors may be less habitual but still predictable since the antecedents and consequences of such behaviors are known to the behaving person and to the observer. We go to school, work, date, get married, go to concerts, on vacations, raise children, etc. Although predictable and socially acceptable, these behaviors do not always have survival value nor are they always conducive to growth.

There are other types of behavior for which the antecedents are obscure both to the observer and the behaving person; such are, for example, the person who gets angry at someone else without a valid reason or the individual who is never able to get angry; the woman who consistently engages in sadomasochistic relationships; the man who is lonely yet cannot get close to anyone or show any tenderness; the graduate student for whom it is so important to do well and cannot study, etc. They are not aware of the factors that have determined their choices to be angry for no reason or not to be angry when such reason exists, not to engage in healthy mutually enhancing relationships, to stay away from people and remain stern and aloof, yet so lonely. These choices, often destructive, are made for reasons not available to the individual's awareness.

For the purpose of this discussion, we could make a crude and limited analogy between a human being and a computer. In the same way as a person has to make constant choices and decisions, a computer is called upon to provide answers to questions. The odds that the computer will provide the correct answers increase as additional data are fed into the computer and correctly programmed. The same holds true with a human being. The more information is available to a person and the more correctly he or she can interpret such information, the greater the odds that the the right decision will be made for that particular person.

To rephrase the above in slightly different terms, we could say that at any given time, the greater the awareness of the factors motivating a decision and of the available alternatives and their possible consequences, the greater the probability that the decision will be conducive to growth.

For the purpose of this analogy, the data potentially available to a person can be divided into two broad categories: data generated from within and data generated from without. The first category would include sensory awareness, both of one's physical self and one's environment. For example, one must be able and willing to see, touch, taste, hear, and smell. One must be able to recognize physical tiredness, tension, pain, or well-being and relaxation. In addition, I will include in that category not only the undifferentiated experiences of well-being, frustration, pain, etc., but also the more differentiated emotions that result from the interaction of these feeling states and the environment such as fear, love, loneliness, anger, joy, jealousy, despair, etc.

Input into the human computer of data generated from without starts at birth and occurs through the process of learning. Some of this learning is carefully structured and acquired through formal teachings, the media, books, etc. Most of it, however, perhaps the most important part, is acquired through unplanned experiences occurring throughout a person's life, especially as such events relate to interpersonal relationships.

The computer/human organism analogy bears an additional similarity, that of programming. No matter how much data are fed into a computer, correct programming is essential to achieve the desired goal. In the case of a human being, programming may be defined as the manner in which the data were fed (taught) and, therefore, experienced and interpreted. Correct programming is the kind of teaching characterized by acceptance, care, kindness, patience, and respect for the dignity and individuality of the learner, the kind of teaching that allows the learner to accept or to reject without fear new learnings that he or she may find incompatible with the data already available and generated from within.

Ideally a person should be totally aware of the data generated from within as well as from without and has been fed accurate and correctly programmed data. This kind of person, of course, does not exist and that is why our decisions are not always judicious, and our behavior not always appropriate and conducive to happiness and self-fulfillment.*

The obvious question, then, can be phrased as follows: "What are the factors that interfere with a person's awareness, therefore preventing him or her from making decisions conducive to self-growth?"

---

*I should clarify that I am not concerned with learnings acquired in a structured manner through formal academic training, media, books, etc., although, by no means, do I imply that this kind of learning is insignificant.

Such interfering factors are many and not all are known. It is possible, however, to identify three categories of such factors as follows:

1. The information that we obtain from our environment, especially that information which contributes to the image we build of ourself may be inaccurate. We may be told that we are ugly, incompetent, doomed to failure, etc. Such inaccurate information may be accepted as fact and our choices and decisions reached accordingly thus making self-fulfilling prophecies occur, which in turn reinforces our belief in and reliance upon such false data. The following brief anecdote illustrates the manner in which inaccurate information about oneself can be incorporated so strongly in one's self-concept that it may have a deleterious effect throughout a person's life:

> Daniel, a Catholic priest in his early thirties, complained sadly that he had never been able to enjoy a close relationship with another human being. When asked to explain what prevented him from engaging in such a relationship, he said "fear, hopelessness and failure." Listening to group members who played the parts of his fear, his sense of failure, etc., he stated: "You all sound like my father. Ever since I was a little boy, all he ever said to me was 'You'll never make it, you'll never amount to anything. Don't waste your time trying, etc.' Well, I obliged him, here I am and never made it."*

2. Another set of factors that interferes with a person's awareness may be labeled "incorrect programming or bad teaching of correct information." Parental and other authority teachings may be conveyed with anger, derision, punishment, and with no regard for the person's feelings. Such teachings may be rejected, distorted, or, if adopted, result in a distortion or denial of one's feelings (i.e., of the data generated from within). A simple example will make the above somewhat clearer:

*This incident was part of a very involved group meeting that will be described in detail in another chapter of this book.

Johnny, a 6-year-old, is angry at his younger sister who took his toy away and he hits her. Johnny's mother witnesses the incident, slaps Johnny and says "You must never hit your sister again. Only bad boys hit their baby sisters and Mommy does not love bad boys."

The consequences of the mother's behavior are numerous. Johnny may reject and distort his mother's teachings and continue to experience anger and express it in violent and inappropriate ways. He may even accept the definition of himself as "bad," flaunt it, and set about to deserve it fully.

Johnny may accept his mother's teachings and associate expression of anger (hitting his sister) with physical (slapping) and emotional (rejection) punishment. Such overt angry behavior becomes frightening because it is followed by such unpleasant consequences and becomes inhibited. It must be remembered, however, that the angry behavior was preceded and accompanied by the feeling of anger. "Feeling anger" becomes also frightening, and to use a different language, we may say that this feeling becomes a conditioned stimulus to anxiety. In the same way as the expression of anger becomes inhibited, the feeling of anger is denied, therefore rendered unavailable to Johnny's awareness. Later in life, Johnny will not know when he is angry and probably will react inappropriately to situations that should have provoked an angry response. He may allow himself to be taken advantage of, may render people uncomfortable by his everlasting serene attitude and indirect and subtle hostility, or he may develop in the process stomach ulcers and muscular aches and pains.

A more appropriate intervention on the mother's part could have been as follows: "Of course you are angry, Johnny, but do not hit your sister. It hurts her." Johnny could have been taught to differentiate between the covert behavior of feeling anger and the resulting overt behavior, i.e., physical assault. Correct programming would have resulted in Johnny's acquiring the knowledge that it is acceptable to experience anger but that to express that anger via a physical assault may have dangerous consequences for another person who may be dear to us. Such overt expression of anger should, therefore, either be curbed or used with discrimination and caution.

A third set of factors interfering with awareness is related to the hurt that past experiences have caused. The pain could have been physical, emotional, as when something happens to a loved one, or may be related to a threatened self-concept. Because pain is such an unpleasant state, we try, and often manage, to push painful memories and experiences out of our awareness. Yet, our behavior is still influenced by such past experiences. This process has often been described by different authors (Dollard & Miller, 1950; Freud, 1938). Although it would be redundant to dwell on its dynamics any further, two examples will serve to illustrate it.

Sophie was a 35-year-old woman who came into therapy to overcome a fear of flying. Behavior therapy was successful to an extent. Sophie was no longer afraid to fly but was still very uncomfortable while walking through the hallways of the airport, in fact she disliked walking through any hallways. A behavioral approach to deal with such discomfort had failed. Sophie and I mutually agreed to continue therapy using a more psychodynamic, traditional approach. Eventually, she remembered with much affect one episode of her childhood. Sophie was 3 years old when she had her tonsils removed. Her parents were not allowed to accompany her past the door of the operating wing of the hospital. Sophie remembered being wheeled through "interminable" hallways until she reached the operating table and feeling terrified and abandoned. Shortly after that experience we resumed a behavioral approach to treating her discomfort at walking through hallways. This second attempt was very successful.

Bernice was a very attractive, talented, somewhat seductive young woman in her early twenties who was very prone to pontificate and give unwanted advice. Donna, on the other hand, was somewhat older, serious and, although attractive in her own right, tended to dress conservatively and engaged into interpersonal relationships, especially with men, in a cautious and guarded manner. For some reason that had not yet been explored, Bernice and Donna tended to clash quite often. On that day, Bernice had made some innocuous remark to Donna regarding her rather severe hairdo. Donna turned toward Bernice and, with sudden and uncharacteristic violence, screamed at her "Goddamn it, keep your fucking advice to yourself" and, unexpectedly, broke down in convulsive sobs. The group was stunned, almost too frightened to react. I moved over to Donna, put my arms around her and held her until the tears subsided. Donna then shared with us a period of her life that she had never previously talked about. She stated that she had a younger sister who was more attractive and more outgoing than she. Boys always gravitated around the sister, and Donna, feeling left out, was often bitter and jealous. Several years earlier, Donna and her sister had had a violent argument and, the next day, on her way to college the sister had been killed in a plane crash. The day on which the lashing out occurred was the anniversary of her death. As she finished talking, Donna spontaneously reached for Bernice's hand, put it against her cheek and said "God, you are so much like her."

Both Sophie and Donna had pushed painful memories out of their awareness. Sophie did not wish to remember her ride through the hospital's hallways, and Donna did not want to remember her feelings of anger, rivalry, and guilt toward her sister. Their behavior, however, was influenced by such experiences. Sophie had developed an unexplained fear of hallways while Donna's reactions to another group member were inappropriate. In the case of Sophie, reacquisition of the forgotten knowledge made her amenable to a successful psychotherapeutic intervention. In the case of Donna such reacquisition was sufficient to initiate more appropriate behaviors.

Through increased awareness a person can:

1. Acquire accurate information about him or herself
2. Reinterpret and experience in a different way learnings that had either been distorted or had been instrumental in distorting one's feelings and self-concept

3.   Reacquire past knowledges that had been pushed out of awareness

The three sets of factors interfering with awareness are neither independent, mutually exclusive, or always coexisting. Incorrect programming may well result in painful memories and experiences that are pushed out of awareness. It is, sometimes, very difficult to distinguish the results of bad teaching from the results of teaching inaccurate information. This categorization offers a reasonable framework for defining the psychotherapeutic process and its relationship to what happens in group therapy.

CLOSURE*

Let us now assume that, as a result of therapy, maturation, or other life experiences, the person has become increasingly aware of the antecedents and possible consequences of his or her choice, as well as of other available options. The odds for decisions conducive to growth have increased greatly and these decisions have been made, be they to get closer to other people, to avoid confrontation, to assert oneself, to express love, to study for an examination, to look at oneself in a more realistic and positive way, to defy one's parents or accept their dictates, etc. The person is now ready to engage into a new set of behaviors.

New decisions and readiness to engage in new behaviors are often insufficient and no guarantee of follow-through. Whether or not these new behaviors will be engaged in and successfully performed depends on a number of factors, one of them being the person's ability to devote sufficient energy to the

---

*The concepts of *closure* and *unfinished business* have been described by Polster and Polster (1973) and this discussion borrows from their description.

performance of new behaviors. It is a truism to state that this is not always possible. It is possible, however, to help the person increase the energy available for any particular behavior. "Closure," for example, is a factor that makes it easier for a person to carry out new decisions and perform new behaviors in a successful manner by increasing that person's ability to devote more energy to the new task.

The concept of *closure* is somewhat more difficult to describe than the concept of awareness and, here, the human being/computer analogy ceases to be valid. Indeed, a computer does not initiate its own questions while a human being is required to do so. It is difficult to initiate new questions unless and until the previous questions have been answered; it is difficult to carry out new decisions until the previous decision has been satisfactorily carried out. The old decision that has not been carried out, the need that has not been satisfied, the "unfinished business" linger on, intrude into what one is doing, prevent one from devoting one's total energy to the task at hand, thus defeating the successful performance of the new behaviors and the carrying out of the new decisions.

I would like, therefore, to define *closure as the process in therapy (or outside therapy) through which the person is helped to satisfy old needs, and carry out to completion previous decisions, thus liberating his or her energy for carrying out new decisions and engaging successfully in new behaviors.* This definition will become clearer as the process is illustrated in the following examples:

> Michael, a 26-year-old steel worker, expressed his sadness to the group for not ever having been able to feel, let alone express, any affection for his father. His father, 76 and in ill health, was not expected to live many more years. In describing his father, Michael sketched the picture of a hard, brutal, yet lonely man. He had never expressed any affection to any member of the family and seemed totally insensitive to any of their needs. He would occasionally beat his children and was drunk most of the time. With Michael's and the group's consent, the group leader di-

rected a psychodrama during the course of which Michael was helped to become very angry at his father. Instead of being subdued and subtly sarcastic as was his habit in the few conversations he had with his father, he raised his voice, screamed, almost losing control of himself and directed at his father a torrent of invectives and obscenities. When he was spent, he and his father (i.e., the group member who played the part of his father) sat side by side and had a long talk. Michael shared with his father his hurt, his loneliness as a child growing up without a father, his fears, his sadness at his father's impending death. He ended up crying and hugging his father and, the drama having ended and the group having reconvened as a group, he stated "Strange . . . I am 26 years old and it is the first time in my whole life that I became aware that deep there, somewhere, there is still some love for the old bastard" . . . he paused slightly, then added . . . "but I had to wade through all that shit to find out."

It may be worth mentioning that several weeks after that session, Michael sent me a letter, part of which is quoted below:

For some reason, it was easier to me to listen to him. I felt it easier not to cut him off, get up and leave as I had always done since I had grown big enough not to be afraid of him. Somehow, this must have affected him because he became nicer to me and talks more. He is a lonely, lonely old man. We shall never be as father and son, but, somehow, I feel now that we are communicating and it will be O.K. when he dies.

The following episode illustrates a slightly different type of closure:

Caroline, a 30-year-old group member, had been very much involved in the drug scene in the 1960s. In 1966, she struck up a relationship with another addict with whom she had gone to school as a child. They were together as the young man overdosed and died. This was what motivated Caroline to change her life style. She was detoxified, joined AA (Alcoholics Anonymous), eventually married a man with whom she was very much in love and very happy. At the time of this particular session, Caroline had been off drugs for almost 10 years. As she was relating her experience with her boyfriend in 1966, she stated that the boy had a mother who was very fond of Caroline. At the young man's death, his family moved to the Midwest and nothing was heard of them. Caroline never had a chance to see or talk to the mother. Indeed, during the young man's funeral, Caroline was already in the detoxification unit of a hospital. Then, she added, "It has already been ten years and yet, I still catch myself thinking of her and feeling so sad. I know it worries my husband. Strange, why should I think of her and not of him?" At that moment, Betsy a 50-year-old group member, spontaneously stood up, went over to Caroline, put her arm around her and rested Caroline's head on her breast. Caroline burst into tears and her words were hard to hear except for these two sentences that she kept repeating as a leitmotif "I am so sorry ... I am so sorry ... Please, please forgive me." After a while, she calmed down, drew slightly away from Betsy, while still holding her hand, turned to the group and said "I think it will be all right now."

It is evident that closure may be conceived differently. It can be looked at in terms of a hierarchy of needs, be these needs physiologic or simply learned. It is difficult to concentrate when one needs to urinate. It is difficult to enjoy oneself when one has a learned, strong sense of duty and has left a task unfinished. Both needs, that is to urinate and to finish the unfinished task, have to be satisfied before being able to engage wholeheartedly in new endeavors. Closure may be viewed as a process through which one is helped to accept, work through, and integrate past experiences, as was the case for Caroline. It can also facilitate interpersonal relationships by helping the person experience and express a set of feelings thus enabling him or her to become in touch with another level of feelings hitherto unavailable to one's awareness, as in the case of Michael.

REHEARSAL OF NEW BEHAVIORS

Having reached growth-conducive decisions through increased awareness and having managed to free one's energy from the demands of past incomplete experiences is often, but not always, sufficient to engage in new behaviors. It is not always enough to know that we now feel free to confront another person, to express our love, to assert our needs, and to do what we were so afraid to do. We must be shown how to do it so that we can be our true self and, at the same time, be part of others and blend with the human race. We must, for instance, learn to be confrontive and assertive but in a humanistic manner so that we will respect the rights of others and be sensitive to their needs. We must learn to express affection without awkwardness but also without depriving the object of our love from needed vital space. We must learn to perform over and over the once threatening action and persist even though we encounter failure, resistance, and rejection. Only then will these new behaviors become truly part of oneself.

I do not mean to imply that all three processes (i.e., awareness, closure and rehearsal of new behaviors) must necessarily occur in order for therapy to be a successful endeavor. The acquisition of awareness is often sufficient for change and, as behavior therapists have repeatedly demonstrated, rehearsal of new behaviors, under certain structured conditions, is often all that is needed for certain behaviors to be performed successfully. I maintain, however, that the most adequate form of psychotherapy is one that affords the greatest opportunity for these three processes to occur.

It is interesting also that the major contemporary theoretical approaches to therapy differentially emphasize these three processes while recognizing their importance. Psychoanalytically oriented approaches lean toward cognitive awareness while client-centered therapy favors affective awareness. Gestalt therapy accents sensory and affective awareness as well as closure. Behavior therapists, on the other hand, favor practice. They all, however, have many common areas, whether explicit or implicit, and it is important to realize that a dogmatic "either-or" approach is not fruitful and that the field of psychotherapy has reached a degree of sophistication that sees the major approaches converging and drawing from each other (Birk & Brinkley-Birk, 1974; Naar, 1970, 1979; Patterson, 1968; Truax & Carkhuff, 1967). With the above in mind, I would like to briefly compare individual and group therapy within the context of the processes of awareness, closure, and rehearsal of new behaviors.

INDIVIDUAL AND GROUP THERAPY

Awareness

Both individual and group therapy lend themselves to an increase in cognitive awareness. Individual therapy, however, is clearly superior, because the focus of the action is on one person only. Such concentration is much more difficult in a group.

Affective awareness occurs both in individual and group therapy. It has been my experience, however, that it is easier and less threatening to allow oneself to feel in a group than in an individual interaction. Indeed, in individual therapy, the therapist is the only object of concentrated transferences. By virtue of his or her role, the therapist is endowed by his or her clients, for quite a while, with an unrealistic aura of power. Because an overt expression of such feelings as love, hate, jealousy, etc., to authority figures in the past was frightening, experiencing such feelings toward an authority figure in the present (i.e., the therapist) is also anxiety provoking and slow to occur. It is also fair to state that expression of such feelings on the part of the client may also be threatening to many therapists who, consciously or unconsciously, subtly discourage them.

This is also true of group interactions but to a much lesser extent. Group members are usually (although not always) seen as peers. Expression of feelings to each other, although still fraught with the dangers of rejection and/or retaliation, is less frightening and occurs faster and more often. In addition to being less frightening, expressing and experiencing positive and negative emotions is facilitated by the example and the reinforcement that group members give to each other.

Affective awareness is facilitated in groups for another reason. Indeed, while life events vary from person to person, feelings are universal and vicarious experiencing of another person's emotions is a common phenomenon. Who is the group leader or the group member who has not shared in the sadness and sorrow or joy and success experienced by someone else in the group?

Group therapy provides members with an additional kind of awareness: feedback on the impact each has on others. Because the range of behaviors one engages in individual therapy is narrow and because of the therapist's sometimes misguided concern for his or her client's feelings, vulnerable self-concept, and/or the nature of the relationship, such feedback is incomplete and slow in coming in individual therapy. In groups, however, it is always present, sometimes gentle, sometimes direct and frank but, in well-conducted groups, always with tenderness and concern.

It is my belief that sensory awareness increases as a result of increased cognitive and affective awareness.* Yet, if we believe that any interpersonal interaction is instrumental in helping us to know ourselves better, then the increased interaction in group therapy is more conducive than individual therapy to the awareness of one's physical self. Indeed, in individual therapy, physical contact is either nonexistent or limited to a gesture of support at times of extreme stress (Holroyd & Brodsky, 1977). In groups, however, the presence of other people removes many inhibitions and such gestures of affection and support as hugs, putting one's arms around another person's shoulders, holding another person while he or she is crying are common occurrences. While such behaviors sound rather in-

---

*Certain contemporary approaches to therapy such as Rolfing, bioenergetics, and so on claim increased sensory awareness as a direct result of the therapeutic intervention. I have neither the knowledge of nor experience with these approaches necessary to comment on these claims.

nocuous to most people, they often acquire momentous importance for those who have felt isolated, rejected, unloved and unlovable, and become instrumental in helping them get in touch not only with their feelings but with their body as well.

Closure

One can achieve closure in individual as well as in group therapy. Closure is usually achieved verbally and its effectiveness varies according to the nature of the past experience. Sometimes sharing with a therapist what one has always wanted to but never could tell anyone, putting into words in the presence of an interested listener the things that one should have done but never did or should have said but never said is sufficient to lay to rest ghosts from the past. At other times, however, talking is not enough. In the example mentioned earlier in this chapter, it is very doubtful whether Michael could have freed himself from his anger at his father and come in contact with his love, had he not acted it out rather than have talked it out. Talking about an experience provides a safe distancing from the emotions attached to it. While this is often enough, the poignant immediacy that accompanies "acting" instead of "talking about" is essential at other times.

It is somewhat ironic and distressing that the majority of group therapists limit themselves and their group members to the use of verbalizations while the genius of J. L. Moreno (1964) had provided us, so many years ago, with an extraordinary tool called psychodrama as a means, among many other things, to free ourselves from the shackles of the past, to complete the "unfinished business" and reacquire our spontaneity. It is only within the past few years that interest in psychodrama has been reawakened and the mainstream of group therapists is becoming aware of its immense potential. (Psychodrama will be discussed later in this book.) Suffice it to say, at this time, that even though it lends itself to use in a dyadic interaction, it is mainly within the group context that it can be used in its full amplitude, thus providing the group leader with an invaluable tool to achieve closure.

Rehearsal of New Behaviors

Individual therapy is clearly at a disadvantage when it comes to practicing new behaviors. Indeed, the narrow range of behaviors possible in an individual session, the artificiality of the situation, the definition of the therapy situation as that involving a therapist and a client or patient, make it very difficult, often impossible, to engage into certain behaviors.* Confrontation, listening to and giving feedback to others, expression of affection and support, receiving affection and support, overt anger, etc., are grist for the group mill.

I stated at the beginning of this chapter that . . . "it is possible to make a case for the preferred use of groups on theoretical grounds by agreeing upon a definition of psychotherapy and deciding which of the two modalities, individual or group therapy, comes closer to meeting the definition agreed upon . . ." It would have been more accurate to state ". . . which of the two modalities, individual or group therapy as I practice it . . ."

Indeed, as my definition of therapy is, I hope, logical, yet arbitrary and idiosyncratic, so is the way in which I practice and teach group therapy. The reader must keep in mind that there is nothing sacred in my pronouncements and that one has to develop one's own style within the context of one's knowledge, personality, and philosophy of life.

---

*Even though many of us would prefer to eliminate the therapist-patient distinction, that definition is nevertheless reality bound (see Szaz 1961).

Chapter 2

A THEORETICAL FRAMEWORK FOR GROUP PSYCHOTHERAPY

Group psychotherapy is not a new phenomenon; the term was coined by Moreno as early as 1932. Yet it is only in the past 15 years that it acquired a new impetus as traditional approaches were joined by more innovative, albeit not always more effective (or even as effective), methods. The many contributing factors to this resurgence of group psychotherapy included a greater awareness of psychological maladjustment and the possibility that something can be done to alleviate it, the advent of community mental health centers, and the humanistic facets of the civil rights and antiwar movements that put many of us in touch with our own alienation. For whatever reasons, groups have mushroomed in the past several years; these include therapy groups, sensitivity groups, encounter groups, analytically oriented groups, workshops, labs, and so on.

The dearth of trained professionals and the unfortunate contemporary stance marked with concern with "what works" and little interest, if any, for "why does it work" were responsible for a painful confusion among group leaders (Patterson,

1968). Too often, the past several years witnessed a blissful disregard for the consequences to patients of charismatic techniques used without understanding of their effect and without being steeped in theory (Naar, 1979). The painstaking efforts at theoretical underpinnings of the early pioneers (Bion, 1972; Slavson, 1950; Moreno, 1964) were not followed through in recent years. With the notable exception of Yalom (1978) the attempts at steeping the modern practice of group therapy into a cohesive theoretical framework have been fragmentary and the state of the art can still be accurately reflected in Kagan's (1970) following statement.

> It seems to me that the encounter group is a therapy without much of a theory: a powerful tool guided by not well-explicated concepts. We need to create or discover more precise, accurate terms and concepts if we are to explain and guide more reliably the process and outcome of counseling groups.

Indeed, while theoretical underpinnings are believed by many not to be essential to leading a group, whatever the nature of the group, a loose, theoretical structure offers not only some guidance and security, but also the possibility of formulating hypotheses that could later be tested experimentally. In this belief, I submit the following propositions as a broad and open-ended theoretical framework. Before embarking upon this task, however, I wish to clarify the following points about my own propositions.

1. The concepts and ideas expressed are not original; they were borrowed from many sources: Carl Rogers, Fritz Perls and his disciples, learning theorists, as well as group leaders who have led groups that I attended.
2. This framework does, in no way, negate other theoretical approaches. It has, however, been found useful to account for what occurs in the kind of groups described in this book.

3. The reader may feel that the last part of the theory
    pays inordinate attention to what happens to persons
    within the group rather than to what happens to the
    group. This observation is, indeed accurate. I believe
    that the group is a tool, a powerful and beautiful tool,
    but not an end in itself. The end (a poor choice of
    words because it is an ongoing process) is the lives of
    the people who form the group.

THE THEORY*

Assumption I: *Every person is potentially capable of making
decisions conducive to growth. Such decisions are reached and
implemented when one or more of the following processes occur:*

1. The decision has been reached on the basis of accurate,
    sufficient, and correctly conveyed and interpreted
    data. For the purpose of developing this theory of
    group therapy, I will call possession of such data
    "awareness." The process necessary to reach growth-
    conducive decisions is that process leading to greater
    acquisition of data or "increased awareness."
2. Previous related decisions must have been carried out
    to completion, that is, *closure.*
3. The new behaviors needed for the implementation of
    the decisions reached must be learned through, some-
    times, repeated performance. This is rehearsal of new
    behaviors.

I believe that increased awareness is at the basis of the
changes occurring in therapy and, although discussed at length
in the preceding chapter, the factors interfering with its acquisi-

*This theoretical framework borrows heavily from Rogers theory of
personality and behavior (1951).

tion bear summarization. These factors, inaccurate data, data inaccurately taught and interpreted, and/or insufficient data are briefly discussed below. As these factors are dealt with and corrected, awareness grows.

1. Inaccurate data

Inaccurate data are transmitted directly or subtly, usually by authority and parental figures, and usually relate to a person's self-concept. A child who has been made to believe that he or she is unintelligent and incapable of achieving may decide not to apply for college admission even though he or she may have more than the necessary intellectual ability. This decision will be logical, but it will not be growth-conducive because it was based on inaccurate information, e.g., "I am not intelligent."

2. Data inaccurately taught and interpreted

This process is somewhat more difficult to conceptualize and may be broken down into the following three steps. A concrete example of how this process sometimes operates was provided in the preceding chapter (see the case of Johnny).

1. Overt expression of genuine feelings, both positive and negative, can be inhibited if followed by noxious consequences such as punishment, disapproval, rejection, withdrawal of love, ridicule, etc.
2. Overt expression of genuine feelings is preceded by an experiencing of such feelings.
3. The experience of feelings becomes anxiety producing (since it was usually followed by an overt expression that in turn was followed by punishment). Because anxiety is an unpleasant state, the person attempts to reduce it. He or she does so by not allowing the feelings to reach awareness. As a result, such persons do

not act upon these feelings, but instead adopt other modes of coping with their environment. One may remain inappropriately gentle and understanding while, at the same time, indirectly and subtly hostile; another person may be remote and distant and build a wall around himself or herself. Another may become overly dependent and ingratiating. Whatever the mode of adjustment, it is assumed that much energy is expended in keeping these feelings out of one's awareness, an energy that could have been used for more constructive ends. Even if one is not willing to accept the concept of a finite amount of psychic energy transferable from one task to another, the fact remains that the persons described above function defectively by not being angry and assertive when anger and assertiveness are called for, by depriving themselves of the warmth and support of interpersonal relationships, by their inability to be independent and self-reliant, etc. It is also worth noting that such behaviors, i.e. inappropriate meekness, subtle hostility, distancing or overdependency, may bring forth negative reactions from those with whom one interacts. These negative reactions further reinforce one's isolation and poor self-concept.

3. Insufficient data

The concept of "insufficient data" is used here in a narrow sense and refers to past experiences and knowledges that, at one time available to the individual, have been pushed out of awareness because of the pain they have caused.

Assumption II: *There is in every person a drive to explore and seek information from his or her psychological and emotional as well as physical worlds.*

The assumption of such a self-exploratory drive is necessary to account for the initiation and maintenance of the person's behaviors leading to increased awareness. It is really not a novel concept but merely an expansion of Fowler's (1965) treatment of exploratory behavior which states:

> With a view toward the 'mechanics' or 'workings' of exploration, it would seem from our review of the literature that we are justified in promoting two principle tenets: whether through high drive or high arousal, the organism is motivated by exposure to homogenous, simple, restricted, and/or redundant stimulation; correspondingly, it will respond to and learn to work for stimulation that reduces its drive or arousal—that is, stimulation that is novel, unfamiliar, complex, and/or changing. If we are to summarize these two tenets in a few words or with a single picture, then that picture is one of the organism *needing, seeking, and processing information,* not in the sense of receiving signals or stimulus input, but in the full theoretical sense of the word (p. 73).

In humans, an exploratory drive may be inferred from the person seeking information not only from the physical but also from the psychological and emotional environments. Information from the psychological and emotional realms is provided in the form of thoughts, feelings, memories, self-awareness, etc. Any behavior, therefore, which tends to seek and process such information (i.e., gradual awareness of feelings, uncovering of memories, elicitation of feedback from others about oneself) reduces the exploratory drive and becomes self-reinforcing (Naar, 1970).

The concept of "self-exploratory drive" is also related to Rogers' theory of motivation. In his chapter on a theory of personality and behavior, Rogers (1951) postulates that "the organism has one basic tendency and striving—to actualize, maintain and enhance the experiencing organism (p. 490)." He states:

> We are speaking of the tendency of the organism to move in the
> direction of maturation, as maturation is defined for each spe-
> cies. This involves self-actualization, though it should be under-
> stood that this, too, is a directional term ... The organism
> actualizes itself in the direction of greater differentiation of or-
> gans and functions. It moves in the direction of limited expan-
> sion through growth, expansion through extending itself by
> means of its tools and expansion through reproduction. It moves
> in the direction of greater independence or self-responsibility (p.
> 491).

I conceive the self-exploratory drive as one aspect of the organism's maturation and self-actualizing behavior. Through the acquisition of increased awareness, the person truly moves in the direction of greater independence and self-responsibility.

Assumption III: *The group is a forum that affords an opportunity for achieving the three goals of therapy provided certain conditions are present.*

The noxious consequences of expressing oneself honestly and openly must be eliminated. Feelings and thoughts, no matter what they are, are accepted with respect although not always with approval. The group milieu must be one of trust, support, and utmost respect for each member's freedom and right to be oneself without fear of being rejected, belittled, or ridiculed.* Obviously, it is sometimes difficult to reconcile honesty and support. A supportive group is a group that will rally around a member in distress, not to fight that member's battles, but to convey to him or her that the group can be leaned on if he or she chooses to do so. A supportive group is one in which group members will not be afraid to reveal aspects of themselves that they had felt were unacceptable. A supportive group is not one that will shy away from confrontation or give blank

---

*"To be oneself" has become somewhat of a cliché. Within the context of this discussion, to be oneself is to be aware of what one is feeling and thinking and able to express such feelings and thoughts in an appropriate and humane manner.

approval to every member's behaviors. Honesty calls for confrontation, disagreements, and, sometimes, painful feedback,
which must be expressed with care, humanity, and respect for
the person's dignity. It is incumbent upon the leader to establish
and promote a milieu characterized by both honesty and support. This will be discussed at greater length in a later chapter.

The concept of a supportive group, one where "the noxious
consequences of expressing oneself openly and honestly are
eliminated" is crucial and pivotal to the theory because without
it, open and honest expression cannot occur. It may be helpful
at this point to cite the comment of a group member as well as
a moving incident that occurred in a group. Both the comment
and the incident illustrate how a supportive group is perceived
and how a supportive group makes its presence felt while leaving to individual members the choice to use or not to use the
available help. The comment was made by a 29-year-old
woman who said "The group is like a womb and you are all like
blood vessels. I feel support and strength flowing from each of
you to me. When I leave here I always feel that I can cope better
and the day will come when I won't have to come back."

Nancy, an attractive 42-year-old, had managed to overcome a
deprived childhood and the early death of her mother, had raised
a much younger sister, and put herself through college and
graduate school. She had married a man with whom she had
spent some very miserable years and had divorced him shortly
before the group session during which this incident occurred.
Nancy, who had been with the group for several months, arrived
at the session and, contrary to her usual behavior, greeted no one
and sat in silence. (The group room had no chairs but comfortable pillows on the floor.) After some superficial exchanges, a
group member turned to Nancy and asked if something was
wrong, and, in a very flat tone of voice, Nancy informed us that
she had been to two physicians and that both had diagnosed
breast tumors and suggested a double mastectomy. The group
was stunned. After several minutes of silence there was a warm
outpour of sympathy, concern, and expressions of sadness and
fear. Nancy remained immobile and silent, impervious to what-

ever was being said. I reflected on Nancy's silence, stating that sometimes the hurt is such that it numbs. The group became silent again. After several minutes, I remarked that there is nothing more frustrating than to witness such a frightening thing happen to a person close to us. I also wondered what fantasies each of us might have regarding the fact that we all were vulnerable. My comments had no effect on the silence. After a while, it felt as if the group were descending into a spiral of depression and I decided that some action, in addition to just dealing with the group process was called for. The following interaction took place:

Therapist: You know, Nancy, life is sometimes like Penelope's tapestry. Do you remember the legend of Ulysses and Penelope? He was gone to the wars of Troy and when he did not return, the courtesans wanted Penelope to remarry. She accepted but asked them to wait until she finished weaving her tapestry. She, then, would spend her days weaving and, at night, would get up and undo her work of the day. You busted your ass getting through school, raising your kid sister, putting up with all that shit your husband had been giving you for years and now that you can see daylight and are beginning to enjoy life, this is what happens.

Nancy: (Nods in silence)

Therapist: You know what I want to ask you to do? Imagine that all those who undid your tapestry are, there, on that pillow, fate, doctors, illness, husband, whatever. Talk to them and tell them what is going on inside you right now.

Nancy: (In a very low tone of voice) I feel . . . I feel I want to talk to my mother.

Therapist: Go ahead.

Nancy: Mom, Mom . . . I need you. Why did you leave me? Why? I need you so much . . . (her voice trails off and stops).

Therapist: Nancy, I feel . . . I feel like this very minute you wish you were dead.

Nancy: (Nods)

Therapist: It's all right, Nancy. Why don't you go into that corner and let yourself die for as long as you want to. Then, you will be ready to come back to life and you will join us.*

---

*Any variations of a scene involving the protagonist's death are potentially dangerous and should be used with great caution. This will be discussed at greater length in the section on special issues.

Nancy: (She stands up, goes into a corner, and rolls herself up into a fetal position.)

By that time, dusk had come and no one had made an effort to turn the lights on. The group members silently began to move and formed a tight ring around Nancy. No one said a word, no one reached for or touched her. It was as if by some miracle of subliminal communication, they all sensed that Nancy had to taste alone the depth of her loneliness and despair before being able to recognize and accept love. After what seemed to be an eternity but was, actually, no more than 12 to 15 minutes, Nancy raised her head and was startled by the physical closeness of the group. She was directly facing a male member; he almost instinctively opened his arms and Nancy flew into them and burst into sobs. The other group members gathered around, put their arms around her and held her and rocked her like a baby. After a while, the tears subsided, Nancy smiled and said "I'm all right now, I am fine." A pall of gloom seemed to have been lifted and the group settled to discuss Nancy's condition in a practical and matter-of-fact fashion. (*Note*: Nancy, upon the advice and with the encouragement of the group, went to a nationally known specialist. Her breast tumors turned out to be benign and Nancy did not have her breasts amputated. While I do not wish to make a dogmatic cause and effect statement, I wonder if Nancy would have been motivated to seek a third opinion were it not for the session that lifted her out of her despair.)

The group waited until Nancy was ready for their support and their support was the crucial factor that helped her emerge from her depression.

A model to pattern oneself after should be available. Indeed, even if one is motivated to explore and express oneself openly and even if such expression is accepted and rewarded, this is often not enough. The person may have never engaged in such behaviors and really not know how or may not have engaged in them for such a long time that he or she has forgotten how to do so. It is not easy to confront, to express love, to show fear or admit to weakness. Unless one sees how it is being done, it may take a very long time, if ever, to find out that it is safe to do so.

At the beginning, the model is provided by the leader who must be courageous enough to share his or her feelings. This is not easy in many respects. In the first place, a competent leader must be capable of experiencing, be in touch with his or her feelings, have enough self-knowledge to recognize transferential feelings when they occur, be willing to get close enough to the clients in order to share nonpublic aspects of the self. Obviously, a competent leader needs much more than academic knowledge; to be a model is difficult from a technical point of view as well. How much can a leader share and at what pace can he or she share so that he or she will not frighten the group members but remain a model to be imitated? When should a group leader refrain from sharing himself or herself so that the members of the group will feel neither imposed upon, nor crowded out of the scene by a narcissistic leader? How can a group leader be open and sharing yet convey to the group members the feeling that it is all right not to do so until one is good and ready? All these points will be discussed later within the context of the leader's role. *For the purpose of this theory of group, suffice it to say that the availability of a model is a necessary condition for certain events to occur in group therapy.*

When the two conditions described above exist (i.e., an accepting and supportive milieu and an available model) the following events may occur:

1. Each group member, gradually and at each one's pace, arrives at the realization that the noxious consequences of expressing oneself honestly and openly are indeed eliminated.

> Jonathan, a third-year resident in radiology, had come to group after being unable to cope on his own with painful bouts of anxiety and depression. His decision to come into therapy was protracted and difficult because he considered it a sign of weakness and failure. He attended several sessions, remaining silent and withdrawn. Eventually, he spoke and said "It is hard for me to understand how you can talk about yourselves in this way. In a way, I guess, I look down on you as I look down on myself for being here. Yet, I wish I had the courage to talk like you do."

2. The group, receiving the group member's communication, gives some kind of feedback. When the communication is genuine and open, the feedback is positive. Jonathan's communication was received with the following statements:

> Jane: It must have taken a lot of courage to say what you just said.
> Michael: It pisses me off to hear things like that and, then, I remember that that's exactly how I felt when I first came to group. So, hang in there, old buddy. You'll do all right.
> Sue: I don't agree with you, but I'm glad you talked. I feel like I know you better. I kinda feel a little closer to you, not so remote as before.
>
> At a subsequent session, Jonathan confided to the group that he had been quite shaken by their comments. He said "I thought you were going to bite my head off and ostracize me. I couldn't understand how you could still be so nice after what I had said."

3. The group's reinforcement of openness leads members to reaching for increased awareness and encourages them to deal with unresolved conflicts. This process can often be painful and distressing. There is an increased willingness to remember previously repressed painful memories and to deal with unfinished business and unaccomplished goals. This is gratifying in that the drive for self-exploration is reduced. It is often also traumatic in that the original pain is reactivated. Again, the support of the group is very important at such times. Without it, the reactivated pain, often, would have been stronger than the gratification derived from the self-exploration.

> Guillermo, a South American scientist in his late forties, was an attractive, intelligent, and sensitive person. He had joined a group for a number of reasons, one of them being a need for closer interpersonal relationships. He was supportive of others and conveyed a feeling of strength and self-sufficiency. He had occasionally talked of the terrible relationship he had had with his mother but, somehow, always stopped short of being specific

and becoming emotional about it. The group respected his reticence in as much as Guillermo was usually a very open person. One evening, he stated "My mother is sick and may die soon and I've got to talk about her." As he was unraveling the horrible saga of his childhood he burst into tears and, after he finished, he added "I wanted to talk about this for years but there was no one I could talk with except you. I knew you would understand and that it would matter to you."

4. *Pain and/or stress experienced by a group member elicit feelings of sympathy, affection, and support from the rest of the group. These feelings are expressed by the group and received by the group member in distress.* While it is very meaningful to a person in pain to receive positive feelings, expression of such feelings is no less important to those who express them. To express affection and support can be, for some people, even more difficult than to express anger. Indeed, there are few experiences as painful as having one's love rejected. When one is hostile and/or confronting, rejection and retaliation are expected and are part of the game. To experience one's gift of love rejected and unwanted is like the negation of one's self. To give love to someone who needs it and is ready to accept it is a safe and most rewarding experience.

5. *Acceptance of one's real self (i.e., pain, anger, expressions of weakness and affection) by others results in increased self-acceptance and unrealistic, and defensive ways of coping with one's environment as well as with one's feelings are gradually discarded.*

Suzan was a very beautiful and talented woman in her mid-twenties. Raised by parents alternating between being overexacting and over-protecting, she had a very poor image of herself, no faith at all in her abilities, and coped with stress in a little girl manner by being petulant, ingratiating, dramatic, and seductive with the men in the group. The feedback she received from the group was negative and, at times, very painful. Suzan remained in the group, however, because, as she put it many months later

"Every time you laid it on me, I sensed your concern and that, somehow, you didn't dislike me. I remember the first time I tried to stop playing my little girl's games—which I didn't even know I was playing—you made such a big fuss over me that for the first time I thought 'Hey, I can stand on my own two legs and still be liked. I don't have to be a baby.' "

6. *Discarding old and unrealistic coping mechanisms liberates energy that is used to more constructive ends and better functioning.* The person is now free to become angry and assertive when anger and assertiveness are called for, is no longer afraid to engage in warm and meaningful interpersonal relationships, no longer afraid to be independent and self-reliant.

Suzan, for instance, became less concerned with pleasing her husband by conforming to all of his wishes, and asserted herself much more in their conjugal relationship. Initially confused by his wife's change, Suzan's husband agreed to see a marriage counselor. Two sessions were sufficient and his respect for his wife greatly increased and their relationship was strengthened and became much deeper. Suzan's career with a television station became increasingly successful in that she no longer shied away from new assignments. She was able to demonstrate her truly enormous talent in her field, and was adequately appreciated. Less dependent, less demanding, she made new and good friends outside the group.

She had become capable of meeting reality without compromising the integrity of her real self as she had done for so many years.

As Hall and Lindzey (1957) have pointed out there is nothing sacred about a theory. In developing the above framework, I have attempted to account for what happens in group therapy in a succinct and logical manner. I have attempted to build upon propositions already tested and accepted by others and to use concepts that potentially can be defined operationally. My hope is that, someday, an interested reader will test some of this theory's propositions, thus enlarging our knowledge and leading, perhaps to a new, more succinct, more elegant and more encompassing framework. This is how knowledge grows.

It may be worthwhile now to briefly summarize the main tenets of this theory.

SUMMARY

ASSUMPTION I: Every person is potentially capable of making decisions conducive to growth. Such decisions are reached and implemented on the basis of increased awareness, closure, and practice of new behaviors.

ASSUMPTION II: There is in every person a drive to explore and seek information from his or her psychological and emotional as well as physical worlds.

ASSUMPTION III: The group is a forum where the three goals of therapy, i.e., increased awareness, closure, and practice may be attained provided that the noxious consequences of expressing oneself honestly and openly are eliminated; and a model must be available to pattern oneself after.

When the above two conditions exist the following events may occur:

1.   Each group member, gradually and at each one's pace, arrives at the realization that the noxious consequences of expressing oneself openly and honestly are eliminated.
2.   The group, receiving the group member's communication, gives some kind of feedback; when the communication is genuine and open, the feedback is positive.
3.   The group's positive feedback encourages members to seek increased awareness and to deal with unresolved

conflicts. This process can sometimes cause pain and distress.

4. Pain and/or stress experienced by a group member elicit feelings of sympathy, affection, and support from the rest of the group. Two categories of important events occur. These feelings are expressed by the group and received by the group member in distress.

5. Acceptance of one's real self by others results in increased self-acceptance and unrealistic and defensive ways of coping with one's environment as well as with one's feelings are gradually discarded.

6. Discarding old and unrealistic coping mechanisms liberates energy that is used to more constructive ends and better functioning.

Chapter 3

THE PROCESS

A controversy often encountered in the group therapy literature as well as in discussions among group therapists has to do
with whether one should concentrate on the group or on the
individual within the group. Other ways in which the argument
is couched are in terms of process versus content or in terms
of a horizontal (what happens in the here-and-now) as opposed
to a vertical (what happened in the past) dimension. Durkin
(1972), for instance, states:

> But a sharp difference of opinion arises when we examine the
> latter *(i.e., the forces which tie the group together).* Analytic
> group therapists view the components of the group consistently
> in the dimension of time and depth, while group dynamics and
> communications therapists prefer to deal exclusively with the
> here-and-now, to rely on observable behavior alone rather than
> the less exact process of inference upon which the concept of
> unconscious infantile motivation depends (p. 163).

It would seem, at first sight, that the argument is specious.
Indeed, a group is made of people. They, not the group as an

abstract concept, are important. On the other hand, the fact that their interaction occurs in a group setting affects their behavior and, ultimately and hopefully, their life and happiness. Yet the dichotomy of the group versus the individual, and of process versus content persists. The divergent views are well-illustrated by the Tavistock approach on one hand with its exclusive emphasis upon the group themes, and the Gestalt approach on the other with its minimization of the interactions between group members and its focusing on the therapist-group member dyad.

As pointed out by Horowitz (1977), group therapists eventually make their own adjustment and develop their own style, remaining somewhere between the two extremes, according to their training, philosophy, and personality. Such adjustment, however, takes time and experience, and, while it occurs, causes much discomfort especially in beginners who tend to vacillate between focusing on the group and focusing on the individual.

I suggest that a group therapist should be well-trained both in group and individual dynamics. He should be able and willing to deal both with the group and the individual within the group, to weave in and out of the process, to shift from one dimension to another according to the needs of the group, and the needs of the individuals who form the group. This suggestion is illustrated in the following anecdotes. The first example illustrates a shift from the needs of the group to the needs of the individual.

> During the preceding session, Carol, a popular member of the group, came in unusually agitated and under very obvious stress. She stated that something terrible had occurred between her and her husband and that she needed to talk about it. Much as she liked and trusted everyone in the group, however, she felt unable to share what had happened. As the group was attempting to offer some support, Carol wondered whether it would be all right to just talk separately to two members to whom she felt particularly close. The group assured her that it would be OK and that no one would mind.

During the next session, the members of this unusually close group sat some distance apart from each other and, after a fairly long silence, began to discuss superficialities in an awkward manner. I asked them if they would try to get in touch with what was happening at that very moment, both in terms of their feelings and their interaction. Some of their comments were: "I feel lonely and alienated from the rest of you." "I feel very tense." "We are bull-shitting a lot." "Something is the matter but I don't know what it is."

The group kept at it and, eventually, tied the process to what had happened the previous week. They owned up to their feelings of anger and rejection while Carol acknowledged that she had felt guilty and miserable all week. The two members to whom she had confided the previous week also shared their ambivalent feelings about that session. As the interaction progressed in a more heated and open manner, the group members moved physically closer to each other and the initial tension and awkwardness seemed to dissipate. There was another period of silence. The quality of that second silence, however, was different from the first as illustrated by a member's comment: "I am glad we talked about it. I feel a lot more relaxed."

At that moment, another member, Michelle, stated, "I need your help, folks. I have an important problem I want to talk about but I couldn't do it when we came in." The group, then, spent the next 45 minutes helping Michelle with her problems.

The nature of Michelle's problem is not relevant to this discussion. The point I wished to illustrate was that Michelle had not felt comfortable sharing her problem with the group until the tension and awkwardness felt by the group was dissipated. The needs of the group were prominent at the beginning of the session and blocked the expression of the needs of individual members. It is only after they were dealt with that Michelle could state her problem. At that moment, the focus of the action shifted from the group to Michelle.

The following anecdote illustrates the manner in which a group can shift from one dimension to another, namely from the present to the past and vice versa.

Bob, an attorney, who had joined an ongoing group, was there for his first session. Arriving directly from his office and not really knowing what to expect, he was formally dressed with coat and tie, wearing a hat and carrying a brief case. The norms of that group were such that group members were almost always casually attired. Mark, another group member, addressed to Bob several sarcastic and hostile comments wondering "where the hell did he think he was? A God damn tea party or something?" etc. His outburst shocked Bob, and the other group members came to his rescue, stating that while they were somewhat amused, they were not angered by Bob's appearance. Thus confronted, Mark admitted that his reaction might have been exaggerated. He insisted, however, that his feelings were quite genuine and wondered about what there was within him that made him react so strongly, yet inappropriately, to Bob. With the group's assistance, he became aware of a similarity between his feelings toward Bob as he had entered the room and his feelings toward his older brother whenever that older brother was praised by their father. According to Mark, his older brother was the father's favorite and, somehow, always managed to do better than Mark in school and other activities. "He was" said Mark, "always so neat and well-dressed while I looked like a bum ... in fact, I had made it a point to look like a bum just because he always was so duded up ..." At that point, at Mark's request and with the consent of the rest of the group, we set up an elaborate psychodramatic encounter. During that encounter, Mark became very angry at his father but also experienced some very tender feelings toward his brother and became aware of the possibility that his brother may not have always enjoyed their father's affection, and, perhaps, not actively sought it out. When the drama ended, Mark stated that his anger toward Bob had dissipated and he felt very good about having him in the group.

In order to more fully explore the role of the leader in weaving in and out of the process, moving from one dimension to another, and shifting between the needs of the group and the needs of the individual, the therapist must define the concepts of "here-and-now" and "process" and show how they relate to each other.

The "Here-and-Now"

Although "group process" may be understood in several ways, there is general agreement among group therapists as to the meaning of "here-and-now".* Within the context of this book, the "here-and-now" is conceptualized below. Interpersonal communication is, of course, a major variable in group therapy. Group members react to each other at different levels, one of which is a feeling level. Members may feel affection, fear, dislike, compassion, and jealousy for each other and may experience a need to confront, to challenge, to support, etc. At a later stage, these feelings are expressed behaviorally and their legitimacy is sometimes questioned and explored as were the feelings of Mark toward Bob in the preceding vignette. (Ways in which to deal with transferential feelings will be discussed later within the context of the leader's role.) To be in the "here-and-now" is to be aware of such feelings as they occur and, when appropriate, to express them. To avoid the "here-and-now" is to block, deny, or avoid such feelings as they occur.

Marge, a 25-year-old woman, had attended eight to ten group sessions. Impulsive and with a poor sense of timing, she had the habit of interrupting other group members quite inappropriately. She would go into meaningless tirades having little to do with what was happening at the moment. One evening, toward the end of the session, she was confronted quite forcefully by the group. Marge became angry, burst into tears, and stormed out of the room. An uneasy silence followed but not much could be said since the time had come to a close. The following week, Marge did not appear. The group's interaction was awkward, superficial; verbal and nonverbal communication were stilted and without spontaneity. At that moment, the group was avoiding the "here-and-now" in that it was not dealing with the feelings of anger, guilt, and sadness as well as with the fantasies stimulated by Marge's absence. Later during the session, after

*For a discussion of the "here-and-now" concept as understood by various schools of group therapy, see Shaffer and Galinsky (1974).

the group leader pointed out their unusual behavior, group members began to express their feelings regarding Marge's absence but deliberately chose not to discuss Marge's behavior and the events of the preceding session until she came back. Their attitude changed, became more relaxed, their interaction more personal and more emotional. They were back in the "here-and-now."

The "here-and-now" concept encompasses more than just its one aspect described above. Indeed, group interactions can be moving, tremendously important to a person, even instrumental in changing the course of that person's life. The life of that person, however, occurs outside of the group. It unfolds within the group for a limited time, but has begun and will end outside of the group setting. Death of loved ones, the birth of a child, encountering one's companions, decisions affecting one's future, successes, and failures, all occur outside the group. To focus exclusively on what happens in the group is superficial, unreal, and unnecessarily restricting. Events that occurred at another place, memories and happenings of long ago may still be very much alive, may still hurt, may still be "unfinished business" preventing a person from growing and marching on. Or, a person may be bursting with an unexpressed feeling of joy and happiness that he or she desires to share with people who care. To share these emotions, be they positive or negative, to express feelings still associated to past events and memories in an open and genuine fashion is also living in the "here-and-now." On the other hand, to talk about things that happened at other times, at other places as a defense against dealing with sometimes unpleasant or frightening feelings and happenings occurring within the group (e.g., confrontation, termination, anger, sadness, love) is a cop-out, an avoidance of the "here-and-now." Perhaps an example will better illustrate the meaning.

The group was silent. The preceding week had seen a confrontation between two members that had made the rest of the group quite uncomfortable. The session had ended without the group working through the discomfort. The heavy silence of the next session was broken eventually by Christine. She remarked casually that she had run across a friend whom she had not seen in a long time and commented on her new hairdo, on what she had been doing and so on. She went on for a while and when her comments fell flat and brought forth no response from the rest of the group, she shrugged and said "Oh, well, I really did not care about her anyway."

In her attempt to alleviate the anxiety occasioned by the latest conflict between the two group members and by the ensuing painful silence, Christine was actually running away from it by dealing with something that had happened outside of the group and at another time. She was avoiding the "here-and-now."

In that same group, at another time, David walked in quite excited and, with a great deal of feeling in his voice, described how he had run into an old army buddy whom he had not seen in many years. His joy and excitement were evident and the group warmed up to him, shared in his pleasure and in some of his nostalgic memories and, after a while, went on to another topic.

Even though David was talking about something that had happened outside of the group and at another time, his feelings were sincere and genuinely expressed. Such expression was not an attempt to run away and avoid something else happening in that group at that moment. He was, indeed, in the "here-and-now."

One additional point remains to be made before closing this discussion. Humans are thinking as well as feeling organisms. It is true, of course, that thinking and expressing thoughts verbally is a much less threatening activity than feeling and expressing feelings. Intellectual behavior is more acceptable in our culture than emotional behavior and almost any forum is appropriate for it. It is also true that a therapy group is one of the few places where honest expression of emotions is learned and encouraged. It is, nevertheless, as undesirable to suppress and stifle thoughts within the group as it is to suppress and stifle feelings outside the group. People, even in a group, occasionally wish to engage in intellectual discussion. It is only when such intellectual exchanges are used as a defense against dealing with what happens in the group that they qualify as an avoidance of the "here-and-now."

The same is true of levity. Occasional good humor and fun, when not used as an avoidance mechanism, can be very much part of the "here-and-now." Thinking and laughing are important aspects of being human. A group that remains constantly at a feeling level and looks down upon thinking and laughing can be very dull indeed.

THE GROUP PROCESS

In common parlance among group therapists, a "process group" is one where the interaction is genuine, open, and at a feeling level as opposed to a group where the interaction is defensive, closed, and at an intellectual level. A cursory review of the literature reveals some consensus but no clearly shared definition of group process (Cox, 1973; Durkin, 1972; Sager & Kaplan, 1972; Wise 1977). The definition and discussion of this concept, as offered here and as it applies to the group as well as to the people within the group, are no more adequate or complete than any of the other interpretations found in the literature. They are useful, however, in understanding the practice of group therapy described in this book.

I define process as "the manner in which things happen." This rather simplistic definition suggests a number of corollaries:

1.   The nature of the "things" is not relevant. What matters is how they occur. A "thing" may occur spontane-

ously (in the sense that the triggering mechanism is not known). It may occur as a response to an identified triggering mechanism. It may occur as the result of the interaction of two or more "things."

2. "Thing" may be defined in many different ways according to the nature of the field of study.

3. Not only is energy necessary for a process to occur but whenever energy is generated a process occurs. Process stops only when there is no energy.

In the field of natural sciences, "things" are defined as elements. In the field of psychology, "things" are defined as behavior whether overt or covert (i.e., thoughts, feelings, etc.). In group therapy, "things" are defined as communication. Therefore, for the purpose of this discussion, the above definition is refined as follows: *"Process" in group therapy is the manner in which communication occurs.* Again, this definition suggests a number of implications.

First, there is always an ongoing process. Even when the group members are totally silent, something is going on. The group may communicate fear, resistance, peacefulness, expectations, etc.

This particular group had recessed for the summer and had reconvened the first week of September. Two new members had been added. The first 15 minutes were painfully silent. Through this silence, the old group members were communicating reentry pangs, resentment at the two new members, and a reluctance at openly expressing these feelings. The two new members were communicating apprehension, expectations, and a resistance at becoming involved. All of the above feelings were communicated through silence. Silence, therefore, was the process. It should be added that, in that particular instance, the process was not very effective. Eventually, however, as the session progressed, many of these feelings were expressed openly. The last 5 minutes of the session were also spent in silence. A group member then stated "It feels good to be back" and the others nodded. A second member turned to the newcomers and said "Welcome to the

group and I really mean that." The communications expressed
were relief and contentment. The process was silence followed by
short verbalizations.

Different messages can be communicated in the same manner, that is, through the same process. This was illustrated in the preceding example where communications as diverse as resentment and contentment and apprehension and relief, were expressed through silence. On the other hand, the same message can be conveyed in many different ways. For example, a handshake (an expression of friendship) can become a robust hand clasping, a clammy and lifeless touching of hands, or the complicated ritual popularized by black Americans in the 1960s. The communication is "an expression of friendship" while the process is the "type of handshake" used. From this point on, to avoid confusion, the intended communication will be called "content" while the manner in which that communication is conveyed will continue to be referred to as "process."

Process and content occur at many levels, i.e., the level of the individual, the level of a dyad, and the level of the group. Content in the individual is defined as the communication that the individual conveys to others; in the case of a dyad, content is defined as the communication exchanged between two people. In the case of a group, content is defined as the communication that the group as a unit conveys to itself as a unit. The definition of process remains the same at all three levels, i.e., the manner in which communication is conveyed. Process and content at all three levels are illustrated in the following:

Joe came to the session still angry at the group for some comments that had been addressed to him the preceding week; he sat apart from the group, scowling, and tight-lipped. The content was anger. The process was Joe's attitude, sitting arrangement and withdrawal.

Anne, a 25-year-old woman, was whining and complaining about many unfortunate happenings in her life. After listening for a while, Florence, almost twice Anne's age, became very angry at her. In a loud tone of voice and without mincing her words she told Anne what she thought of her continuous whining and complaining. Anne became enraged at Florence's criticism and for a few minutes, the two women screamed at each other. During the ensuing heavy silence, Florence suddenly said "You are such a beautiful girl and you have so many years ahead of you. It breaks my heart to see you make your life so miserable." Anne burst into sobs. Florence went over, slid on the floor next to her, put Anne's head on her breast and rocked her for a while. Anne stopped crying and the two women held hands and smiled at each other. The content was anger, loneliness, sadness, love, and trust. The process was verbal (words and loud tone) as well as nonverbal (embrace, hand-holding, smiling, and moving within the room).

The leader of that particular group was a talented social work student who had completed her one-year internship. She and the group had been together for approximately 10 months and the fact that she would leave at the end of August was known to every group member from the beginning. When she reminded the group that she would be leaving in three weeks, the group's communication became disconnected. Several topics were tried briefly and discarded such as what does a social worker do after graduation, the institution's insensitivity to patients' needs, the new unknown group leader, etc. The content was sadness, affection, feelings of rejection, anxiety, and anger. The process was a verbal exchange of meaningless subjects and an avoidance of the "here-and-now."

It is evident, by now, that the intended communication is not always identical to the communication actually conveyed. Whether or not the "content" is clearly and unambiguously conveyed depends upon the manner in which it is conveyed, i.e., upon the process. In the context of this discussion, a constructive and effective process is one that conveys an intended communication clearly and unambiguously. The more effective the process, the clearer the intended communication.

This is illustrated in the three examples cited above. In the case of Joe, his behavior (silence, sitting arrangements, etc.) was reasonably effective yet could also have been interpreted in different ways. A truly effective process would have been a more direct and open expression of anger. The process was quite effective in the case of Anne and Florence. Their feelings were expressed in a clear and unambiguous manner in terms of the words used, the tone of voice, and the nonverbal exchanges. On the other hand, the process was totally ineffective in the case of the group. Indeed, the communication conveyed (comments on the work of social workers, the attitudes of the institution) seemed, on the surface, to have little to do with the communication intended (i.e., sadness, anger, feelings of rejection, etc.)

It is also evident that the nature of the group and the purpose for which it is formed will determine the kind of content exchanged as well as the process that can more effectively carry that content. For example, in a group of military recruits learning to dismantle and fire an automatic rifle, the content is straightforward information regarding the nomenclature of the various parts of the weapon, the manner in which they fit together, and the way in which the weapon is fired. An effective process may consist of lectures, demonstrations, and clear answers to pertinent questions. In the case of a therapy group made of people whose purpose is to acquire increased and more accurate information about oneself, to complete unfinished business from the past, and to rehearse new behaviors, the content consists mostly of information about oneself, of feelings and thoughts as they keep occurring. An effective process may take several structural forms, such as words, demonstrations, motion, nonverbal exchanges, drama, etc. In addition, however, it must have certain characteristics that are nonessential to a group of soldiers, for example, are indispensable to its effectiveness in a therapy group. Such characteristics include trust, care, mutual respect, openness, honesty, support, directness, sensitivity, etc. An effective process is also characterized by the communicator's awareness of the communication that he or she wishes to convey such as a clear conceptualization of thoughts and the ability to experience and label feelings.

A process characterized by the above is, of course, a goal that occurs only gradually. At this point, it is appropriate to look at what makes a process ineffective and nonconstructive.

The communicator may lack the knowledge necessary for effectively transmitting the communication. He or she may not have acquired an adequate vocabulary and may have difficulty expressing thoughts and feelings.

> John was a sensitive and intelligent young man who experienced the difficulty described above; he had a very hard time ending a sentence and, even after having conveyed his message, would carry on interminably using occasionally pedantic and unusual (albeit appropriate) expressions, to the increased irritation of the group. He was firmly, but gently, confronted with the above tendency. Over time, the group took pains not only to point out to John the instances when he allowed himself to be verbally carried away, but they also taught him to talk more effectively. For instance, they made an effort to listen more attentively, to respond and to congratulate him whenever his communications were short and to the point. When John terminated at the end of two years and said his goodbyes, the comment most often heard had to do with how moving and effective he was when he talked.

The ineffective process may, at one time have served a defensive purpose and, later in the communicator's life, may have become a habit.

> Sister Sarah was part of a group that had begun to meet shortly after Vatican II. Vatican II had set in motion a process that, to a large extent, revolutionized customs and habits among religious people. At one point, during a session, Eleanor, another group member, was sharing with great affect, a very sad event in her life. The other group members, with the exception of Sister Sarah, gravitated toward Eleanor. Sister Sarah remained straight and rigid on her pillow [We used large pillows on the floor instead of chairs.] The group was so involved with Eleanor that Sister Sarah's behavior remained unnoticed. Suddenly, she stood up and, in a loud tone of voice, exclaimed "that is silly," went

over to Eleanor, put her arms around her and told her how much she liked her and how affected she had been by what Eleanor had shared. Much later, she explained to the group the meaning of her exclamation. Indeed, when Sister Sarah was a novice, expressions of affection, especially of a physical nature, were much frowned upon, and Sister Sarah still found it difficult to express positive feelings even though that behavior was now encouraged by the Church. That realization had hit her when the group surrounded Eleanor and her "that is silly" was her way of asserting her freedom from old habits.

The ineffective process may still serve as a defense against real or fancied dangers or against dealing with painful feelings or issues. This can be illustrated in the case of a group which, instead of dealing with the sadness of a tragic happening, talks about superficial matters. It can also be illustrated by the behavior of Tanya, who was so afraid that people would reject her if they knew her, that she was constantly antagonistic, abrasively pushing other group members away while being lonely and sad.

Needless to say, clear categorizations are seldom possible and an ineffective way of conveying a communication may indicate a lack of verbal ability and, at the same time, serve as a defense against imagined dangers stemming from one's early experience. Indeed, a common thread runs through all ineffective processes. In addition to impeding communication, ineffective processes serve a protective purpose. It is good to remember that, sometimes, that purpose has to be respected. Tearing away the protective cloak too fast may well injure an individual's dignity and self-respect. It is also advisable to keep in mind that although the person and/or the group are sometimes aware of the ineffectiveness of the manner in which they communicate, more often than not that awareness is not present.

Much has been written regarding the many different ways in which the person, the dyad, and the group protect themselves by disguising and/or distorting intended communications. Patterns of ineffective processes at all three levels, i.e., the person, the dyad, and the group have been ingeniously detected, described, and labeled (Berne, 1964; Bion, 1972; Freud, 1954). These patterns recur, and a group therapist should be able to recognize them. One should be wary, however, of labels and categorizations and resist the impulse of trying to fit all ineffective processes into an identified category. I believe it is more important to understand what the intended communication really is, how it threatens the communicator, and how the ineffective process attempts to ward the threat. It is more important to feel the intensity of the fear and the intensity of the need to communicate than to know the correct label to attach to a process. This understanding comes to a group therapist partly through readings and to a greater extent through time and experience, in particular through his ability to listen, to experience with, to participate, to be an integral part of the group microcosm.

One point remains to be made. Sometimes, communications break down and the process lacks effectiveness not because of the communicator's inability to convey that communication but because the person (or persons) to whom it is addressed cannot or are not willing to hear it. This is illustrated in the following excerpt from a group session:

> Lou, a 32-year-old man, was describing with great feeling his encounter with a young woman. Lou was shy and reserved, tended to stay away from people and build all sorts of fantasies around potential but nonexistent interpersonal relationships. In this particular instance, however, he had overcome his shyness. He and the girl had liked each other, spent the night together and made plans to see each other again. As Lou was talking, it was apparent that the sexual encounter was incidental and that his excitement stemmed from the fact that he had not run from a relationship but instead had managed to make something good happen instead of just dreaming about it. At that moment, Buck, another group member, interrupted Lou and related the saga of his first, only, as well as unsuccessful sexual experience in a whorehouse. While his statement was incongruous, there seemed

to be a poignant sadness in his voice. After a few minutes of painful silence, the following exchange took place:

Mary Anne: Buck, sometimes I am not sure I understand you. Like right now, I don't know where you are coming from. But, I know you speak from the heart.

Buck: (in a very low tone of voice): Yes, I do.

Lou: I was pissed, for a minute, there . . . Like you really didn't give a damn about what I said.

Loreen: It's like you are really hurting, Buck, but sometimes, it's difficult to follow you.

Buck: I am hurting! I am 23 years old, and I never screwed a woman and I never will.

Therapist: I have a feeling that you are so wrapped up in that hurt that you are not always aware of what goes on and, sometimes, just a word heard, here-and-there, triggers your pain.

Buck: That's true and people make fun of me. But I don't want to be this way.

Therapist: Would it be all right, Buck, if when this happens here we tell you?

Buck (with tears in his eyes): Yes, please. I wish you would. I trust you people.

Indeed, Buck was so engrossed in his own loneliness that he had not resonated to Lou's happiness. It is evident that Buck was no more skilled in receiving than sending messages and the expression of his loneliness came clothed in a rather gross, somewhat amusing description of a first visit to a whorehouse. This, of course, is not surprising in that in order to hear others one must also hear oneself.

The relationship between the "here-and-now" and the "process" is now clearer. In a therapy group when the content consists primarily of feelings, of information about oneself, and honest and concerned feedback to others, an effective process requires that the communicator become aware of feelings and thoughts and become able to express them as they occur. These very words were used at the beginning of this chapter to define the concept of "here-and-now." An effective process in group psychotherapy requires, therefore, that the people who communicate with each other be able to live in the here-and-now.

How can this be accomplished? How can a group leader help group menbers live in the here-and-now and, thus, promote an effective process? This will be discussed in the next chapter.

Chapter 4

THE ROLE AND TASKS OF THE LEADER

Every group therapist, like every group member, is a unique individual and the groups that he or she leads will bear the stamp of his or her personality. Some therapists are outgoing and forceful, others more reserved and withdrawn; some can make friends easily while others are more distant. In the same way as the individuality of group members is accepted and encouraged, group leaders should be encouraged to grope, explore, and develop *modi operandi,* approaches and techniques that fit their personalities and with which they feel comfortable. Rigid conformity to a model, uncritical adherence to someone's teachings can often inhibit the student's spontaneity and become an obstacle to innovations and new knowledge. Just as group members develop as individuals while pursuing the goals of enhanced communication, increased awareness and freedom from the shackles of the past, so group leaders should find their own style within a framework whose purpose should be to help group members achieve their goals. This chapter and that which follows present such a framework. The concrete techniques described have worked for me. I hope that the reader may adopt some of them, discard some others and, as he or she grows in experience, develop his or her own.

Three propositions central to the group therapy approach described in this book bear repeating. They are essential to an understanding of the leader's role and helpful in introducing what I believe to be, by far, the most important task and responsibility of a group leader:

1. Increased awareness, closure, and rehearsal of new behaviors should be the goals of therapy.
2. The above goals can be reached in a group through clear and unambiguous communication (i.e., an effective process) and the resolution of conflicts (i.e., dealing with the content).
3. Open communication and conflict resolutien are possible in a group milieu characterized by trust, support, and respect for each member's freedom and right to be oneself.

It was stated in the second chapter of this book that the "concept of a supportive group, one where the 'noxious consequences of expressing oneself openly and honestly are eliminated' is crucial and pivotal to the theory since without it open and honest expression cannot occur." Because of the pivotal function of the supportive group, the leader's role in promoting such a milieu is considered to be his or her most important task and will be discussed first.

PROMOTION OF A CLIMATE OF TRUST, SUPPORT, AND MUTUAL RESPECT

The leader of a therapy group acquires, especially at the beginning of a group, an enormous importance to group members; to some extent, this importance is legitimate. Indeed, the group therapist charges for his or her services and is expected to possess a knowledge and expertise that enables him or her to help those who seek such services. To a large extent, however, such importance is exaggerated in that group members, at least initially, endow the leader with qualities, characteristics, and powers that he or she is far from possessing. While the reasons for the real or fancied importance of the leader are not relevant to this discussion, it must always be kept in mind that group members are sensitive to and affected by the leader's behavior to a much greater extent than by the behavior of other group members. The awareness of the leader's importance will make the following concrete suggestions more understandable.

The leader should avoid any verbal and/or nonverbal behavior that tends to belittle, ridicule, or humiliate group members. This guideline sounds superfluous. Indeed, would a group therapist in his or her right mind belittle or humiliate group members? Hopefully not. At the same time, there are many subtle, often unconscious ways in which people can be belittled and ridiculed. The most effective, and perhaps the most painful, is to be ignored; not to ignore a group member does not mean that the therapist should respond constantly to that group member's statements. Indeed, when the process is satisfactory and group members are actively involved with each other, the wise leader keeps silent unless called upon to participate by the group. To not ignore a member means to be actively aware of his or her presence, to listen, to resonate at some level. One's body posture, a gesture, a glance can often be tell-tale signs of the leader's attention. Such attention is important to group members. They are encouraged to continue communicating and feel validated by a person they have cast, at least initially, into a role of importance. To be ignored can be devastating not only because of the dynamics between leader and group member but also because the event occurs in front of other people. The shakier the ignored member's self-concept, the greater the odds that he or she will feel ignored and rejected by the group and, accordingly, increasingly hurt. To interrupt inappropriately, to leave the room without an explanation, to change the topic before it is exhausted are other ways of ignoring a member.

On the other hand, it often happens that a group member can be boring either through the content of the communication or through the ways in which such communication is transmitted. At such times, the leader cannot fake interest. A faked attention is quickly detected and can be more damaging than being ignored. In such instances, the leader should first allow some time to lapse in the expectation that the feelings of boredom will be echoed and verbalized by the group. To give the group a chance, of course, is a cardinal principle although sometimes narcissistic or anxious therapists are quick to preempt group members and to take the initiative. In this instance, to allow the group time to react serves the additional purpose of obtaining a validation of one's feelings of boredom. If the group, however, does not come through, it is incumbent upon the leader to share his or her feelings with the group, try to understand them and, if appropriate, point out to the group member what aspects of that member's behavior triggered boredom. This must be done with great caution, however. The therapist must at first be reasonably certain that his or her feelings are indeed caused by the group member and, such being the case, must provide the feedback in a manner that is both honest and supportive. While this will be discussed further within the context of how to encourage appropriate feedback, the following anecdote illustrates the point.

Jennifer, a 42-year-old extraordinarily talented classical pianist, was somewhat shy and introverted. She used her music as a means of escaping from frightening interpersonal relationships. She was often chided by group members for being a "piano rather than a person." When relating her experiences at a performance or an audition, she would do so in an irritating drone, intermittently detailing technical aspects of her performance. After a while, it became apparent that the group was becoming tense, fidgety, yet, for several minutes, remained silent and made no comments. During a lull in Jennifer's monologue, the therapist said "I wonder if we could take a minute to get in touch with what we are experiencing this very minute." Before anyone had a chance to answer, Jennifer started again.

Therapist: Jennifer: I shall interrupt you for a minute and share with you and the group what I am now experiencing. I caught myself drifting off while you were talking. I wanted to pay attention to what you were saying but couldn't do so. Perhaps I am in one of my off days or perhaps my feelings are shared by others. Let me check this out.

At that moment, other group members came forth and shared their own boredom and frustration. They gently confronted Jennifer with the fact that, even though she was obviously talking about very important things, she was being impersonal, technical, sharing little of her real feelings, and was doing so in such a monotone voice that they could not bring themselves to be attentive.

While the kind of feedback described above may be painful, it is most often accepted and integrated when delivered with care and compassion. In addition, it must be remembered that even negative attention is more constructive and meaningful than no attention at all.

The leader should avoid implied, subtle, or overt rejection of group members who choose to remain defensive and uninvolved. The leader should recognize that people move at different paces.

It is difficult, if not impossible, for a group leader not to become ego involved in the process. Better adjustment and a happier life for the people who seek his or her services are, to a great extent, a therapist's raison d'être. Yet, such adjustment and happiness occur mostly outside the group and are not witnessed by the therapist. The therapist can only rely on verbal reports and on the client's open communication and resolution of conflicts in the sessions. It is a logical inference that, if a group member communicates openly and works on his or her problems, he or she is nearing the goals. When such communication occurs within the group but one group member, through protracted silence, avoids seeking answers to troublesome problems, it is easy for the therapist to feel like a failure, let down, perhaps even betrayed. Even when the therapist wishes to avoid pressuring group members into a specific kind of behavior, he or she may subtly, somtimes unconsciously, ignore, and/or reject shy, withdrawn, and defensive group members. Such rejection may often become a self-fulfilling prophecy in that the group member's shyness increases, and he or she may become even more frightened and defensive. It may push the group member out of the group and, in some extreme cases, may even damage his or her self-concept. A group therapist should recognize that people move at different paces, that some are more verbal and/or more trusting than others; the therapist must also remember that some people can be helped substantially by the group milieu even with minimal involvement as illustrated by the following example:

> Yvette was a very talented artist who taught art in the city's public schools. She disliked teaching and had always had fantasies of earning a living selling her canvasses and of entertaining a meaningful relationship with a man. Having been with the school for years, however, Yvette had tenure and a relatively high salary. Tenure and salary represented a financial security which, understandably, she was very reluctant to forego. Yvette had a beautiful and interesting face with jet black hair, violet eyes, very white skin, and a radiant smile. She was, however, extremely heavy, indeed quite obese. She used her weight as an excuse to avoid socializing and, indeed, her shapeless mass did keep suitors away. Yvette remained with the group for almost two years, hardly saying a word or two per session. Initially, the group confronted her with the feelings that her silence elicited and made repeated but fruitless attempts at drawing her in. Eventually, the group gave up, its anger disarmed by Yvette's unalterable gentleness and the obvious fact that she was always listening and paying attention to what was happening. One day, Yvette requested a leave of absence from the group but refused to explain the reasons for her request. Three months later, she

returned. We all gasped, hardly recognizing her. She was bronzed, slim, elegantly dressed, strikingly beautiful. She explained that, over the years, she had saved several thousand dollars and had spent a good part of her money spending these three months in what she called a "fat farm" in California. She had resigned her job and obtained a part-time position as a clerk with the State Government and was moving to the State's capital planning to devote the rest of her time to painting. Several months later, I ran into Yvette again. She had remained as slim and beautiful as when she had returned from California, was engaged to be married, and actively busy with her painting. On her last night with the group, she said: "You thought I wasn't getting anything out of the group and you were feeling bad about it. It's just that I couldn't talk. Just being here with you, just knowing that you cared for me even though I stayed like a dummy week after week did something to me. I think you gave me the strength to do what I did."

Obviously, not all silent members derive as much benefit from a group as Yvette did and ways to deal with silence as well as with different kinds of difficult members will be discussed in a later chapter. Suffice it to say that, at times, group members listen to their own drum beat and their right to do so has to be respected.

The leader should avoid applying pressure upon group members to conform to his or her standards. It would be redundant to dwell upon the fact that each group leader has a particular style of leading a group. The style is quickly perceived by the group and standards and norms are often built around the leader's style. An aggressive and confrontative style will result in a cowed and inhibited or an aggressive and confrontative group. A leader eschewing confrontation and anger will promote a peaceful but often superficial and bland milieu. The extent to which standards and norms develop around the leader's style depends upon the safety felt by group members. The more they feel accepted and respected by the leader, the more they allow themselves to deviate from his or her norms, and develop their own individual views and styles.

When I first began to work with groups, I quickly became painfully aware of my discomfort at violent confrontations between group members. As I grew in experience, my faith in the strength of my clients grew accordingly and I became less worried at a vulnerability which, more often than not, was fantasy rather than reality. My style is to be gently and supportively honest. At the same time, I no longer defuse confrontations; instead I allow them to happen, careful to avoid scapegoating, and ready to offer some support to a member who might need it. The following anecdotes illustrate how confrontation can be softened without being discouraged.

> Anita, a very attractive Chinese graduate student in psychology, had joined the group after suffering the trauma of a recently broken marriage. It was Anita's first meeting and, after being introduced to the group, she turned to Jerry, a male member, and fired at him numerous pointed questions oblivious to the fact that Jerry was not quite willing to respond. The exchange lasted for several minutes and, without transition, Anita turned to Mary Jo, a shy, withdrawn young woman and bombarded her with personal questions. The following interaction then took place:
>
> Jerry: Are you always like that?
> Anita: What do you mean?
> Jerry: So assertive, pushy.
> Anita: I don't like that word "pushy."
> Jerry: Tough.
> Sheila: Anita, you see that Mary Jo does not feel like answering your questions. Neither did Jerry a while ago; nor would I for that matter. I feel that I would like to know you better before sharing personal things with you.
> Anita: I did not mean to be intrusive. I just wanted to give Mary Jo a chance to say something.
> Therapist: Anita, would you please repeat that last sentence?
> Anita: I wanted to give Mary Jo a chance to say something.
> Therapist: Could anyone spell out the implications of this question?
> Sheila: Of course. It implies, Anita, that you have the power to give Mary Jo a chance to talk and that Mary Jo needs it. That

is a lot of bull. She does not need your permission and you can't
give her anything.

A heavy silence followed. Anita looked angry and defiant.

Therapist: Anita, what did you really mean when you said that
you wanted to give Mary Jo a chance to say something?
Anita: I immediately liked her when I saw her. I felt bad that
she said nothing. I was concerned.
Therapist: You see, Anita, when we want to say something to
another person two things are important: what we want to say,
what is inside us, and how we say it. What was inside you was
very beautiful. The way you said it, however, was kind of pushy
and, if Jerry and Sheila had not pointed it out to you, Mary Jo
would only have heard your intrusive questions and not your
concern.
Mary Jo: That's true. I was mad at you at first, but not any
longer. I thank you.
Jerry (with a smile): It's all right, kiddo. We all go through this.
Sheila: Now, I feel that I am beginning to know you a little.
Anita (cries softly): I have been so miserable for these few
months. . . .

She proceeded to share with the group the pain of her
broken marriage.

On the other hand, an aggressive group leader, whose
aggression is not tempered by care and warmth, may intimidate
the members of a group and coerce them into submissive conformity. The norms may become either frightened withdrawal
and defensiveness or excessive confrontation and anger at the
expense of a wider range of more gentle and loving, yet no less
real, feelings. When the aggressive and uncaring group leader
also displays a certain amount of charisma, the results can be
quite frightening. Indeed, there is a tendency to pattern oneself
after a charismatic leader and the unfortunate group member
who happens to displease him or her incurs not only the leader's
wrath but also that of his or her clones. I witnessed that process
once several years ago and shall describe it as a very unpleasant
experience in a group.

A well-known visiting therapist led a two-day marathon group in which I participated as a member. Halfway through the first day, the leader confronted a young seminary student with what he felt was "his phony helpfulness to other group members." Before the young man had a chance to reflect upon what was a fairly legitimate criticism, he was set upon by four or five other group members who were trying to imitate the leader's style and mannerisms. The attack was rather vicious and soon the young seminarian broke down in convulsive tears. The attack ceased and the young man quickly forgotten, continued to cry alone while the action moved on. Driving home that night, I felt vaguely dissatisfied and knew that my dissatisfaction came from the fact that I had not intervened and was unsuccessful in my attempts to rationalize my lack of intervention. Although I felt no particular liking for the seminarian nor any inclination to fight his battles, these were not the reasons why I had remained silent. Humiliating as the realization was, I had kept silent because I was afraid to become the next scapegoat. I resolved to waste no time in sharing my discovery with the group next morning. Then, the thought made me chuckle. Indeed, that was a way of warning the group of my vulnerability and of asking them not to attack me. I felt amused as well as angry at myself. The next day, there was a repetition of the scene of the preceding session. The next victim was a young woman who also broke down in sobs, unable to withstand the onslaught of the pack. Not without some trepidation, I moved next to the young woman and put my arm around her. For reasons I did not understand until some time later when a group member told me that I looked fierce and ready for battle, the pack made no comment. To his credit, the therapist at last became aware of the young woman's distress, ceased his attacks, and proceeded to give her some additional support. Years later, I ran into that same woman again, and she confided that the experience was one of the most painful in her life and, since that day, she had never attended a group again.

The nature and extent of the leader's confrontative and supportive attitudes are not, of course, the only leader-related factors that affect group norms and standards. The leader's attitudes toward a host of issues, social, political, sexual, etc. may be instrumental in shaping group standards. It could be argued that the leader should keep such views to him- or herself. This is not always possible, especially if the leader wishes to provide a model of humaness and honesty. While this issue (i.e., the leader as a model) will be discussed at length in another section of this chapter, the point to remember is that the leader should always promote a milieu within which the group members can be different, hold and express divergent views, deviate from group standards, and still feel respected and accepted. The two preceding anecdotes provided brief examples of what the leader can do and should avoid doing to create that kind of atmosphere.

Under certain conditions, the leader should encourage appropriate physical expressions of support. The ethics, appropriateness, as well as some empirical findings regarding physical contact in psychotherapy will be discussed later. At this time, I will only assume that some forms of physical contact are appropriate and desirable under certain circumstances. Although it may sound dogmatic, I would suggest that physical contact be limited to holding a person's hand or putting one's arm around another person's shoulder as a gesture of support in a moment of stress; a hug or kiss on the cheek, occasionally, may also be appropriate as an expression of joy, affection, or gratitude.

My attitude toward physical expressions of support may be better understood within the context of the changing culture in the United States. Twenty years ago, physical contact, especially between members of the same sex, was extremely rare, shunned, and often considered rather improper. It was somewhat sad to witness fathers and sons, or close friends, embarrassed and tense at times when aware of affection for each other. It was almost incongruous to see them limiting the display of such affection to a handshake or a fake punch on the arm or the shoulder. Several years ago, while attending a group as a member, I remember the leader asking who, in that group of forty people, felt comfortable expressing affection through a physical gesture. Two of us answered in the affirmative and both had been raised outside of the United States. I remember experiencing a feeling of emptiness at scenes of separation in movies. Later, while serving in the Armed Forces, that same emptiness was present when I would witness families of my friends visiting and then leaving with tears in their eyes but without embracing. It was as if the tears in the corners of their eyes were only partly because of the pain of separation but to a large extent because they could not do what they really wanted to do. They could not share their love for each other in a complete manner.

The 1960s witnessed a healthy change in the above attitudes, and physical expressions of affection and support became much more acceptable. As the prevailing cultural norms are reflected on television, for instance, it is now quite common to see fathers and sons embracing, and friends even of the same sex exchanging a bear hug. In some circles, however, the pendulum swung to the other extreme, and physical contact became a ritual rather than the expression of affection and/or support that it is meant to be. This ritualistic use of physical contact robbed it of its significance. Occasionally, it was even worse. It was not rare to see people take advantage of the new norms in order to obtain personal physical gratification while others for whom meaningless physical contact was distasteful subjected themselves to it for fear of being different or of being rejected.

The three following principles that govern my attitude toward physical contact can now be better understood.

1. Physical expressions of support and affection are desirable and should be encouraged. Indeed, they represent an important mode of communication of which people should not be deprived.
2. Such expressions should be limited in scope as described in the first paragraph of this section. More extensive physical contact could easily become erotic and be used for the sexual gratification of the giver

rather than being an expression of support and/or affection to the recipient.

3. Physical (as well as verbal) expressions of support and/or affection should be used only when they are meant and never in a ritualistic, mechanical, or manipulative fashion.

The above points will be discussed in greater detail in a later chapter. At this time, the role of the leader in promoting the kind of atmosphere where appropriate physical expressions of support can be given and received comfortably and without fear will be discussed.

In spite of the changing cultural norms discussed above, to be touched can still be frightening. Yet, when one is lonely and afraid, when one feels unloved and unlovable, to be touched can be the life saving bush stopping one's fall into a precipice.

Touching someone else can be even more terrifying. Indeed, one's touch can be rejected, and there is hardly a more painful experience than to have one's love spurned. This rejection can be particularly traumatic if the giver feels insecure about him- or herself and not very worthwhile. It does not help much to have an intellectual realization that the rejection is caused by fear and not dislike or disinterest. The pain is hardly alleviated. Even though the norms are changing, to reach for someone else can still be a risky and scary adventure. At the same time, however, it can still be a marvelous, exciting, and rewarding challenge.

> The group, that evening, was in a somber mood, and suicide was the topic of conversation. To various extents, most group members owned to having entertained, at one time or another in their lives, fleeting fantasies of self-destruction. Patrick, a group member in his early forties, who had remained silent until then, spoke one single sentence "I still do." The group was jolted. Indeed, Patrick, a much liked member of the group, was a priest. Under the group's gentle probing, Patrick revealed his extreme loneliness, his tiredness at having to do so much for so many while

there was no one he could turn to, no shoulder he could lean on, no one with whom he could be weak. The group's verbal expressions of support seemed to serve no purpose. Patrick accepted them with a sad little smile that bespoke gratitude. It was evident, however, that all the group's efforts were in vain in shaking his feelings of loneliness and futility. It was one of these rare times when the "content" of the interaction could not be dealt with by the group, and I decided to take an active part in what was happening. The following interaction, then, took place:

Therapist: Patrick, I would like you to imagine that you have died.* Lie down here and put your hands on your chest. (The therapist lowered the rheostat light and group members appeared as vague shadows.) We, the rest of us, are having a wake and mourning Patrick's death.
Tina: Why would he want to die? He had so much to live for. So much to give.
Joe: I am going to miss him so much.
Jane: Whenever something would bother me, whenever I felt hopeless, it was enough to know that he would be here and I'd immediately feel better.
Tina: We all loved him so much.
Liz: But we never really told him.
Therapist: Liz, if by some miracle, he could come back to life, would you tell him?
Liz: (cries, then in a very soft voice) Yes, I would.
Therapist: Try it.
Liz: (She kneels by Patrick, raises his head and holds it against her chest, gently rocking it, crying and saying over and over again) We love you, Patrick . . . we love you.

At that moment, I began to turn the rheostat light up and features again became distinguishable. Patrick seemed transfigured, his eyes wide open and shiny. He was crying and kept repeating as a refrain "They love me, they love me . . . I made this happen, I made this happen . . ." During the preceding scene, Paul, a brilliant, somewhat aloof young man, had re-

*The reader is again reminded that any variation of a scene involving a group member's death is potentially dangerous and should be used with great caution.

mained silent. Paul had been with the group for several months, and although respected by everyone, no closeness had developed between him and the rest of the group. As Patrick stood up, Paul went toward him and, without a word, embraced him. The group was quite astonished because that behavior was so uncharacteristic of Paul. He held on to Patrick for a while then turned toward the rest of us and said, "For a long time, I wanted to tell you all how much you all mean to me but I was afraid that you wouldn't understand." Then, after a moment of silence, he added: "It's the first time in my life that I've hugged a man and, by golly, it feels all right."

(*Note:* Recently, several years after the above group session, I ran into Patrick and told him of my intention to write a book on group therapy. He reminded me of his "death," and asked that I include the episode in the book. He called it a "very important event in my life.")

As for any new behavior with which group members are not accustomed, it is incumbent upon the group leader to provide a model. A few points should be emphasized:

1. The model is provided through the leader's actions and not through his or her exhortations. It is important that group members always feel free to follow or not follow the leader's example without being afraid of rejection or retaliation.

2. The leader must be comfortable with physical contact. Discomfort at touching someone while forcing oneself to do so is always discernible. The gesture of support loses its significance and could even become damaging in that the recipient may lose trust in the therapist. If uneasy with physical contact, the therapist is much better off abstaining altogether. His or her warmth and care, if genuine, will become apparent anyway.

3. Because of the fancied or real importance of the leader as discussed at the beginning of this chapter, his or her verbal and nonverbal behavior acquire much greater significance than that of group members. While not

shirking away from genuine physical expessions of support or affection, the leader must use them sparingly. This point will be discussed further in a later and more extensive section on touching in psychotherapy.

4. The leader must always remember that in nonverbal as well as in verbal communications, he or she must not preempt group members. When group members are initially capable of (or as soon as they become comfortable with) providing each other with appropriate physical expressions of support, the leader must take a back seat and allow group members to take the initiative.

5. There are some very rare instances when active encouragement of a physical expression of support is appropriate. Such encouragement, however, must be given very cautiously, very gently, and only when there is no doubt on the therapist's part that it is desired by the group member.

Francine was a young woman who had recently lost a mother to whom she was very attached and so she spoke of her loss. The intensity of her pain and grieving was evident and moving. Laurie, another woman of approximately the same age, listened intently, bringing her pillow close to Francine's. There were tears in her eyes but she stood rigid, with her hands on her lap. I leaned behind Laurie, took her hand and, very gently, placed it on Francine's shoulder. Laurie turned to me and smiled. Francine reached over her shoulder and held Laurie's hand while she continued to talk. At the end of the session, Laurie, turning to me, said "How did you know I wanted to do that?"

Physical contact, of course, is not always associated with pain and sadness. Affection, joy, gratitude, even levity can be translated in physical exchanges. I have fond memories of clients hugging me and saying "thank you" as they were leaving the group or as a happy event brightened their lives. I always remember the following incident with a chuckle.

Guillermo, the South American scientist mentioned earlier in a different context, was a rather straight-laced and conventional gentleman. Another group member, a lady in her early forties was even more conventional than Guillermo and was very gifted as a raconteuse. She was reporting a rather funny incident with her usual talent and Guillermo impulsively said "This is beautiful. I want to give you a kiss on the cheek." Deborah looked puzzled and said "huh?" while the group burst out in uncontrollable laughter. To fully appreciate the flavor of Deborah's expression and her puzzled "huh?" one must remember that Guillermo's English, although flawless, was quite accented. His "kiss on the cheek" came out as "kees on the chick." Deborah joined in the laughter, and, good naturedly, presented her cheek to Guillermo, a gesture that would have been unthinkable for her under different circumstances.

Joy and levity, sadness, grief, pain, happiness, and affection can all be expressed in so many different ways. We may choose all these ways or only the one with which we feel comfortable. No mode of expression, however, if used appropriately, honestly, and with respect for the other person should be forbidden or avoided; it is also good to remember that the more levels at which a message is communicated, the clearer that message becomes.

François Villon (1952), the French poet and rogue once wrote that no relative or friend can die another person's death. Our death is our own; to a great extent so is our life. This is, perhaps, one of the very important lessons learned in groups. There is a clear understanding that every group member is responsible for his or her decisions and choices and even advice and suggestions are kept to a minimum. The support is not a crutch on which one leans and which may be taken away. It is not an opportunity to unload on someone else one's difficulties. It is a nourishment through which one grows and acquires strength; more accurately, perhaps, it enables people to absorb the nourishment that is there and available. As eloquently stated by the young Israeli girl quoted in a preceding chapter, each member is a fetus fed by many blood vessels. The purpose, however, is to be born and leave the womb. More than any other interpersonal relationship, perhaps in part because they are less fettered by cultural roles and expectations, relationships between group members are uniquely reciprocal. Each group member is a fetus and blood vessel at the same time. He or she feeds and is fed, gives to all and takes from all, and each can say:

> I who give birth to all
> Should be fulfilled by all
> (Moreno, 1941)

THE GROUP LEADER AS A MODEL

One of the cardinal assumptions of the theory developed in the second chapter of this book was that *the group is a forum that affords an opportunity for achieving the three goals of therapy provided certain conditions are present.* One of these conditions is that *a model to pattern oneself after be available.*

The knowledge that it has become safe to engage in new and different behaviors is not always sufficient. Safety has to be experienced, and this is possible only after the new behaviors have been performed without painful consequences. A broken arm continues to be favored long after the bones are healed. The fear of using the injured arm disappears only gradually after repeated use and the realization that the fracture does not reoccur. So it is in a group. Even when one senses that the milieu is one of acceptance and support, that acceptance and support become meaningful only after one has taken the initial risk of revealing a part of one's self and finding that such behavior is not only not punished but also intrinsically and extrinsically rewarding. The initial step is the most difficult to take. Indeed, defensiveness, hiding, isolation, because of the protection that they had afforded in the past, have often become so ingrained that the reversal cannot be started spontaneously.

It is often up to the leader to initiate risk taking, to provide an example, and to show that, indeed, the consequences are not disastrous.

A model is not only needed to overcome fear and gain the realization that the group is truly safe. Even when the individual is intellectually and emotionally ready to engage in new and different behaviors, it may be difficult to do so. Sometimes the different behavior is one in which the person has never engaged; at other times, it may have been so long since the behavior was performed that one has forgotten how. The following utterances are familiar to all group therapists and, common as their occurrence may be, they always maintain their poignancy.

"I don't know how to tell her that I really love her."

"I am no longer afraid of him but I still do what he says . . . habit, I guess."

"I know she likes me . . . but how do you tell a girl you want to go out with her?"

Real life situations such as confronting one's husband, asking a girl for a date, telling one's mother that she is loved, indeed, can, of course, be successfully role played and rehearsed in groups. In addition to the opportunity for role playing such situations, the group offers a unique forum for directly expressing face to face to other people feelings of love and anger, wants, weaknesses, and feelings of sadness. The learning then generalizes to situations encountered outside the group.

Again, it is up to the leader to show how it is done. Through his or her own behavior, figuratively, the therapist gently takes the group member's hand and shows the way to openness. To provide the proper example, yet convey the feeling and the knowledge that group members are free to follow or not to follow that example without fear of rejection or retaliation, is perhaps the group therapist's second most important responsibility. How he or she can live up to it will be discussed below.

Leader's Awareness of and Comfort with his or her Feelings

The therapist, like the clients, is vulnerable to the whole spectrum of human emotions. Some are acceptable and fit within one's image of what a therapist should be; some are less acceptable and clash with the therapist's self-concept. It is, sometimes, painful to come to grips with one's humanness, particularly with what one considers to be weakness and short-comings. Some therapists choose not to feel that pain:

> Joseph was a whining, demanding and self-centered young man in his early twenties. At one time or another, he had exasperated every member of the group and I stoutly maintained to myself and others that I was not irritated by him. (*Note:* Very much a beginner, at that time I had the fantasy of a good therapist as being eternally patient, compassionate, understanding, and steady as a rock.) This went on for several months and I remember being puzzled at a feeling of discomfort whenever Joseph walked into the room. Eventually, Joseph got a job that would have prevented him from attending group sessions. True to his usual behavior, he asked that the group change its meeting time to accommodate his schedule. As I look back, this could conceivably have been done; at least, a good attempt at changing the time could have been made. Instead, I found myself answering very quickly "No, this is impossible." Joseph, of course, left the group. During the next session the interaction was limited and group members seemed to shun me. They were not hostile; rather I sensed some discomfort and hesitation. I was, of course, disturbed by it and at a loss in understanding what was happening. Eventually, the feelings of the group were conveyed to me in the following manner: "We would not have changed the time for Joseph, no way. He was a pain in the ass and we were glad to see him go. But you scared us. There you were, dripping honey for months with him, making us wonder whether we were all crazy or whether you were a blooming saint. Then, out of nowhere, you turn around and don't even give him a chance to check with us. Who knows when you'll turn against us . . ."

Other therapists are more honest, face the anguish but do not know how to cope with it. A young psychiatric resident, leading her first group, describes her feelings as follows:

> I was uncomfortable and upset to feel my eyes filling with tears. I thought that, as a good therapist, I should have felt understanding and compassion, but not be so involved. There I was . . . crying with her. And I kind of felt the almost overwhelming need to hold that child and tell her that things will be all right. That really made me uptight . . .

Another group therapist confides:

> This was the worst session, ever. For some reason, I felt sad. I just was down. And part of me was saying that this was wrong. These people were coming to me to be helped. I literally was feeling guilty about feeling sad. My goddamned jaw hurt from trying to smile.

The ways in which a therapist may cope with his or her feelings and share them will be discussed below. The following brief anecdote can be compared to the episode described above involving Joseph and illustrates how different a reaction can be when the therapist is aware of his or her feelings and attempts to own up to them.

> Richard was a very bright and aggressive young man holding an advanced degree in language communications. It soon became apparent that he was trying to compete with me in the group, assuming the therapist's role, contradicting whatever I would say, etc. His intelligence as well as a certain charm about him precluded his becoming obnoxious and I found myself experiencing my own competitiveness being aroused rather than feeling threatened or annoyed. After two to three weeks which brought no change to the situation, I confronted Richard, saying "I sense that you are constantly trying to compete with me and this makes me feel very uncomfortable. Part of me would enjoy going along with it, because you are so bright and challenging and I

am competitive also. Part of me does not want to because the group interaction would suffer from our game." Richard remained silent for a while, then, more serious than he had ever been, said "O.K., I'll try to control myself but I want you all to help me find out why I always do that and end up making an ass of myself."

Leader's Ability to Express Appropriately his or her Feelings

Awareness of and comfort with one's own feelings is essential but not sufficient. The group therapist must be able to express these feelings honestly and appropriately. To express one's feelings honestly requires a great deal of courage. The therapist must be willing to emerge from the protection of the professional's cloak and to be scrutinized; in a very real sense, he or she voluntarily places him- or herself on the same level as group members, takes chances, and accepts becoming vulnerable. No textbook can teach a therapist how to do that. The courage to reveal oneself can only be learned experientially, acquired through pain, time, faith in oneself and others, sometimes through one's own therapy; to express feelings appropriately, however, can be taught more directly and the following guidelines may be of help.

Intially, the therapist should express his or her feelings honestly but gradually. It should be remembered that to express one's feelings openly is threatening to some people, alien to others, and quite inappropriate to a great many others. Initially, openness is not desirable since its rewarding properties have never been experienced. Witnessing the person to whom one goes for help engage in what one believes to be inappropriate behavior may arouse fears, suspicion, and loss of trust.

During the initial stages of a group, when it is incumbent upon the leader to take the initiative in sharing of him- or herself emotionally, it is important that the level of emotionality be one that conveys accurately what the therapist feels yet does not frighten the group members away. This is how a group member describes his shortlived stay with another group and his subsequent experience with ours:

> I was very nervous as I entered the group. I wished I could fade into the woodwork. I didn't want to have to say anything and I didn't want these people to know anything about me. Then, this girl said something. I was so uptight that I can't remember what she said but it must've been something terrible because the leader started crying and blowing his nose. That did it for me. There was that guy who was supposed to help me put my head together and, boy, he was more screwed up than I. Now, I realize that I was wrong but, at that time, how was I to know. All my life, I had been taught that men don't cry and all that crap. It was like the first time I saw someone eating escargots. He was gulping them down and I thought I was going to be sick. Now, I love them, but it took my wife some gentle persuasion. I remember when I joined your group and I talked about my divorce, your face looked so sad. I know you knew what I was going through but you did not fall apart and I could see the strength in you and I felt safe. Since then, I have also seen you cry, but somehow it has never frightened me.

After the group has been in existence for a while, and it is no longer necessary for the therapist to "show how," it is wise that he or she fade into the background and not preempt group members. The therapist's feelings are important but should come second to the feelings of group members. The principle is cardinal and cannot be emphasized enough. *In a group, the needs of the group members always come before the needs of the therapist.* This principle will be discussed later at greater length. I wish only to comment now upon what "showing one's feelings openly" means and what it does not mean for a group therapist. It means "being one's feelings," i.e., acting sad when one is sad, happy when one is happy, loving when one feels loving. It means that one does not pretend to feel the opposite of what one feels. To "show one's feelings openly" does not mean trooping them forth and imposing them on the group. To be more specific, if I happen to feel sad or happy, I do not begin the session with a display of my feelings but nor do I pretend to be happy or vice-versa as the case may be. If a group member comments upon how I feel, I answer honestly. There is only one exception to the above principle and this exception will be discussed later in this chapter.

Therapist's angry and affectionate feelings toward group members should be expressed with caution. The importance that therapists acquire for group members has already been discussed. Because of that importance feelings of anger and/or affection expressed by the therapist have much greater significance than when expressed by group members. The therapist must, at all times, be aware that the message that he or she conveys may be received at a much higher level of intensity than intended. The dilemma for the group therapist becomes how to maintain his or her integrity and remain genuine while avoiding being misunderstood and damaging the client. It sometimes seems hard to conciliate genuineness and support. It is hard, but not impossible, provided the therapist adheres to certain guidelines:

1.   He or she will not compromise the genuineness of his or her feelings.
2.   Negative and angry feelings can be conveyed in a constructive manner by pairing them with accurate positive comments about the group member. For example "You have a habit of not listening when someone talks and it can be very irritating. Yet, when you take the time to listen, you can be very perceptive and supportive."
3.   The therapist will be specific and make it clear that the annoyance or anger is at the group member's behavior and not at the group member as a person. For example, the therapist may say, "Your whining and demanding manner really annoys me" but should not say "You annoy me."

4. The therapist will take responsibility for his or her comments. He or she may check perceptions against those of the group *if honestly not certain of the legitimacy of his or her feelings,* but will *never* seek group support of a negative feeling against a group member. The therapist may say (if he or she genuinely believes so): "I am annoyed at the way you keep avoiding me. But I am not at all sure that is what annoys me. It may well be something else bugging me today and I haven't figured out what it is. How about it, group? Help me out." The therapist may also say: "I am annoyed at the way you keep avoiding me." The therapist, however, should not say: "I am annoyed at the way you keep avoiding me and I am sure that the group agrees with me."

For many people, anger is not only destructive but irreversible and incompatible with love. An honest expression of anger can be not only a model but also an extraordinary learning experience if that anger is followed by positive feelings:

Several years ago, I was leading an ongoing group of eight Sisters of Charity. The local Diocese had made available to us a beautiful retreat home in the woods for a long weekend. During the morning session, Sister Janet was constantly critical of herself, as well as of the process and the others sisters. Eventually I expressed my irritation in a fairly strong manner. Later, toward the end of the evening session, Sister Janet talked about some extremely painful childhood experiences. There was such an aura of sadness and alienation about her that (I happened to be sitting next to her) I spontaneously put my arm around her and held her for a few seconds. She burst into tears. The other sisters gathered around her, and, as I backed off, provided her with their support. A few days later, Sister Janet sent me a letter, excerpts of which are quoted here: "To some people, it might not seem like much, but to me it was like discovering a new world. There was someone who had been angry at me and yet still loved me. I was not bad, I was not an outsider banished from the inner

circle. Right there and then I made up my mind always to trust
you and the sisters and I'll tell them in group next week."

The expression of positive feelings also requires caution on
the part of the therapist. Hostility, anger, and criticisms hurt
but it is possible to fight back. Tenderness, friendship, gentleness, especially when one is not used to them, disarm and can
make the recipient feel vulnerable and weak. That vulnerability
and weakness can be terribly frightening and one defends oneself against them by rejecting the proferred hand, by answering
gentleness with anger, friendship with hostility. The therapist's
positive feelings should be expressed in such a manner as to be
nonthreatening and not call forth a negative reaction. Further-
more, if the therapist feels that he or she has a difficult time
accepting rejection and feels incapable of renewing an offer of
love after it was spurned, then such a therapist should abstain
from expressing positive feelings. In fact, such a therapist
should seriously consider not leading groups.

Appropriateness of the Therapist Discussing his or her own Problems

Before commenting upon the appropriateness of the leader
using the group as a medium to solve his or her problems, it is
well to differentiate between revealing one's feelings and revealing one's problems.* Open and honest communication requires
that an individual be his or her feelings. As clarified in the
preceding section to be one's feelings means that the person
who feels sad or happy or angry will convey these feelings
through his or her demeanor, posture, tone of voice, or verbally.
Above all, the person will not pretend to feel differently.
Whether or not that person will choose to share specific events
in his or her life, or the recent event that may be responsible
for recent feelings becomes a matter of choice. Withholding

*I am indebted to Walter Kempler, M.D. for his clarification of this
distinction.

some of these events may be a matter of privacy rather than dishonesty. These principles, of course, apply to the group members and the therapist. As far as group members are concerned, however, the distinction between sharing one's feelings and sharing events in one's life is not very important. It is much easier to share happenings in one's life than it is to express one's feelings honestly. The distinction, however, is important in terms of the therapist's motivation in deciding whether or not to share personal problems with the group.

In the early 1960s, especially under the influence of the encounter movement, it was felt by many group leaders that distinctions between therapist and group members should be blurred and that the therapist should consider him- or herself as another group member. The absurdity of this position becomes quickly evident when we recall that the therapist charges group members for services either directly in private practice or indirectly through a salary paid by an institution. The fact that the therapist is paid while the clients pay establishes differential roles. These differential roles will be discussed in another chapter. Suffice it to say that the blurring of roles at times encouraged the therapist to use the group for his or her own end, quite inappropriately and to the detriment of group members. Some therapists have even mistakenly believed that to withhold personal information is a sign of defensiveness or dishonesty. Hence, it is important to make the distinction between revealing one's feelings and revealing one's problems. The therapist must be his or her feelings; one may, however, choose whether and how much to share of his or her personal life and problems.

Another point must be made abundantly clear. There is nothing sacred about the therapist's problems nor do I advocate that he or she never share them with the group. When no one in the group has anything pressing to discuss and a genuine interest is expressed in the therapist, or when the therapist has experienced in the past or is experiencing in the present problems similar to those expressed by the group member and senses that such revelation will be helpful, then the therapist may legitimately verbalize a personal problem. With a single exception that will be discussed below, however, the therapist should abstain from using the group directly as a means of solving his or her own difficulties. This is a matter of ethics, not really a matter of privacy or openness. As stated above, the therapist is paid to help those who pay him acquire greater awareness, put a closure to past experiences, and acquire new behaviors and not vice–versa. Any increased awareness, closure, and new behaviors that the therapist experiences and acquires in the process are fringe benefits. The group members come first, the therapist comes second.

I mentioned earlier that there is one exception to the above rule. *The therapist is justified in preempting group members and in bringing a personal problem to their immediate attention only when such problem is of such magnitude and intensity that it prevents the therapist from functioning adequately.* This exception is dictated by two considerations. The first is that the therapist's inability to function adequately may damage the group members. He or she may not hear accurately what group members convey; he or she may intervene at an inappropriate moment thus hampering the group process. Even worse, the therapist may be unaware of possible stress experienced by group members. The second is that group members, experiencing but not being able to account for the change in the therapist's behavior, may tend to blame themselves and feel guilty, frightened, or resentful, according to each member's idiosyncratic way of coping with the unknown. By sharing the existing problem, the therapist achieves two objectives: the pressure that he or she experiences may be alleviated and, second, the group members will not be confused by and/or blame themselves for the therapist's unusual behavior. Almost needless to say, when such a traumatic event occurs in a therapist's life, it is preferable to cancel the group session. This, however, is not always possible.

Several years ago, approximately ten minutes before a group session was due to start, I received a telephone call from my wife. She had just returned from a gynecologist's office and had been told that she had to undergo an exploratory breast operation. The news was totally unexpected and my psychological state can easily be imagined. It was too late to cancel the group and when the session started, I realized that I was totally incapable of concentrating on what the group members were saying. I told the group that I had something to share with them and explained the situation, apologizing for not being able to pay attention to what was going on. The outpour of support was truly warming, and the group members insisted that I leave and go home to my wife. When surgery revealed only a benign cyst, their joy was no less genuine than their concern. Several weeks later, the incident was discussed again in group, and everyone agreed when a group member stated that the opportunity to help me had been very significant to him. He, then, added, "I am glad you don't have many problems. We need you for ours." The statement was made only half in jest.

The therapist should keep in mind that when a personal problem is brought up under the circumstances described above, the goal is to acquaint the group members with the existence of the problem. It is not to solve the problem. The therapist must choose another forum to solve personal difficulties in the same way as the group members have chosen that particular therapist's group for solving theirs.

Conclusions

Even if the leader was a perfect model, the group members may choose not to imitate him or her. The leader must understand that he or she is simply offering an alternative, a different way to be. The group members are under no obligation to adopt it. They may accept the model *in toto,* reject it, or accept it in part. It is the group member's inalienable right to be what and how he or she wants to be. And when the group member feels free to be him- or herself, free to choose what to accept and what to reject without fear of retaliation and/or rejection, and confident in the acceptance of the group and of the therapist, then the therapist can say "I have done well."

ENHANCING COMMUNICATION AND HASTENING AN EFFECTIVE PROCESS

The milieu is now experienced as safe and supporting; a model for open communication is available in the person of the leader if group members wish to follow it. The stage is set for an effective process to occur. To rephrase the above sentence, the group members are ready to communicate in a manner characterized by trust, openness, honesty, support, directness, and sensitivity.

Theoretically, no further action should be required from the leader. Indeed, it will be remembered that the theoretical framework developed in Chapter 2 included three assumptions and two conditions summarized as follows:

Assumption I: Every person is potentially capable of making decisions conducive to growth.

Assumption II: There is in every person a drive to explore his or her psychological, emotional, and physical environment.

Assumption III: The group is a forum where the three goals of therapy can be attained provided that the noxious consequences of expressing oneself honestly and openly must be eliminated; and a model must be available to pattern oneself after.

By promoting a milieu of trust and support and by being a model, the therapist has fulfilled the two necessary conditions for an effective process to occur. The therapist could legitimately choose to take no further action. He or she could also choose to hasten the occurrence of the effective process by additional interventions. The therapist's decision will be based upon the awareness of his or her abilities, as well as his or her philosophical and theoretical orientation to therapy. Indeed, such interventions are delicate and often demand not only wisdom but also timing, skills, and experience. On the other hand, some therapists possessing the necessary abilities choose not to use them, preferring to rely entirely upon the group members' interactions. It is my belief that additional interventions are desirable; such interventions designed to "enhance the communication and hasten an effective process" will be discussed in this section.

Further Comments on the Nature of an "Effective Process"

The interventions mentioned in the preceding paragraph should, of course, be related to the factors that slow down the development of an effective process even when the necessary conditions of a safe milieu and the availability of a model are present. Some of these factors have already been discussed in Chapter 3. They will again be mentioned briefly to underline the logic of the suggested interventions.

The communicator, be it the group as a whole or a person within the group, may not be aware of what they wish to convey or of the ineffectiveness of the communication process.

Our community was jolted by two successive murders of women in a suburban neighborhood. The group members came in obviously agitated and troubled. For a while nobody spoke, then Dan, in a hesitant tone of voice, brought up the matter. Mary-Joe, an ardent feminist, went into a tirade against men, and Tom, another group member, replied angrily. The argument went on for a few minutes while the other members remained silent.

In another group, Paulette, a verbal and assertive young woman in her late twenties, announced that, feeling much better about herself and all aspects of her life, she was considering leaving the group. She gave herself two additional weeks (i.e., sessions) to mull her decision over and discuss it with the group. Two weeks later she arrived for her last meeting. Frank, a handsome man in his early forties, had remained silent during the group's discussion of Paulette's termination and, as Paulette arrived for her last session, attacked her angrily for what he perceived to be Paulette's "snobbery" and "inappropriate independence" expressed in "wanting to leave the group before she was ready," etc. Frank's outburst was not only inappropriate but also out of character. Indeed, it had been the group's consensus that Paulette was ready to leave, and Frank was a mild, supportive fellow not given to intemperate, illogical attacks on other group members.

The manner in which the above two situations were handled will be discussed later in this chapter.

The "ineffective process" may be a defense. A word of caution is necessary. As repeatedly stated in the preceding chapter, an "ineffective process" is most often a defense. That defense may have served, at one time, not only as a protection against pain, but also as a means of preserving one's pride and dignity. To eliminate it too quickly, before the individual is ready for it, may be not only degrading but also counterproductive. The following comments made by group members illustrate the point.

A 30-year-old physician states: "Initially I had very mixed feelings seeing how easy it was for all of you to share your problems. Even to cry. Part of me was envious and part of me looked down on you. Indeed, to let other people see your problems was a sign of weakness to me. Had you confronted me, with my withdrawn behavior, I'd have been angry, sneered at you, and left the group."

A 27-year-old secretary: "I can't tell you how frightened I was. In fact, I was so scared I couldn't even get up and run. I was so grateful that you let me alone until I was able to get over my fear."

> A 45-year-old man says: "Even when you called me "The Professor" I sensed that you liked me and that it was all right for me to be my usual pompous intellectual 'self.' I am glad I learned, eventually, to talk like a person."

The communicator may have forgotten or may have never learned to convey a communication effectively.

> Marty, a shy, introverted young man, after swallowing hard two or three times, avoiding the group leader's eyes, said in a low tone of voice "I was kinda angry at you last week. You went to the bathroom while I was talking and I felt you really didn't care."

Possible Interventions

As stated in a preceding chapter, an "effective process" is intrinsically and extrinsically rewarded. In an involved and cohesive group, interventions that enhance and hasten open communication initially emanate from the group leader and, eventually, may come from group members. Most of the interventions suggested herein illustrate possible group leader's behaviors.

RETURNING TO THE "HERE-AND-NOW." In a previous chapter, the state of being in the "here-and-now" was defined as an awareness of feelings as they occur and an expression of such feelings when appropriate. Avoiding the "here-and-now" was defined as blocking, denying, or avoiding such feelings as they occur. Such avoidance can, sometimes, be achieved by talking about things that happened at other times and other places. The reader, however, was cautioned against interpreting every discussion of events that occurred elsewhere and at other times as an avoidance behavior. It is only when such discussions are used as an excuse for not dealing with unpleasant or frightening feelings and happenings occurring within the group (e.g., confrontation, termination, anger, sadness, love) that they qualify as an avoidance of the "here-and-now." The same, of course, is true of intellectual exchanges and levity. They become an avoidance of the "here-and-now" when used as a defense against dealing with what happens in the group. The therapist must be able to sense whether they are attempts at not dealing with the "here-and-now." If the discussions are genuine, the therapist's efforts at returning to the "here-and-now" will be in vain since there really is no avoidance. This is illustrated in the following two anecdotes:

The group was a training group composed of professional mental health workers. According to the format followed, two-thirds of the session (80 minutes) were to be a regular group session initially led by the instructor and later by alternating group members. The remainder of the time (40 minutes) was devoted to a debriefing and an analysis of the preceding session. On that particular day, two group members were quite excited over a new approach to family therapy recently published in a journal. After approximately 10 to 15 minutes, I wondered whether we should not leave such an esoteric subject and return to interactions within the group. A brief, awkward silence was followed by half-hearted attempts at focusing on the group members' interactions. Very quickly the conversation drifted back to the topic of family therapy. Obviously, I had not been tuned in to the mood of the group. The interest in the new family therapy approach was genuine and not an avoidance behavior.

In another group, Mike, an emergency room physician, confided that he was seriously thinking of leaving the city and his present job and moving to California. He explained that he had been trained in certain emergency procedures but could not use them because the hospital he was attached to did not handle such "traumatic" cases. Mike liked his colleagues but felt that he was not being used properly and was afraid that he would forget his special training. It should be added that Mike was a popular and well-liked group member. A very open individual, he was sensitive, gentle, supportive as well as direct. It was apparent to me that this unusual interest in emergency room happenings was an attempt at evading the anxiety that his possible departure was causing. Because the group was obviously not dealing with it, I decided to intervene. Several alternatives were available to me. I could have said "I wonder what this interest in emergency room details is all about" or "Let us stop for a second and focus on what is happening now" or I could simply state my own feelings. I chose to do the latter and said "I wish you the best, Mike, but I shall miss you a lot." Emergency room talk vanished and group members shared with Mike their feelings about his possible departure. They were back in the "here-and-now."

A brief digression regarding my choice of intervention is appropriate. The first two choices would have helped the group realize that they were avoiding the "here-and-now" as well as give them some insight on how they were avoiding it. The third statement put the group members immediately in touch with their feelings and back in the "here-and-now." All three interventions are legitimate and each can be rationalized on the basis of the goal pursued by the therapist. In the final analysis, however, the choice made will depend on which approach each therapist is most comfortable with.

There are times when group members are quite aware of what they are experiencing, do not wish to avoid communicating, yet remain silent. The silence may be due to the intensity of the feelings experienced, sometimes to the belief that such an expression may be intruding upon another person's time or feelings. At such times, some encouragement from the therapist may be appropriate. A simple comment such as "What are you feeling just now?" can help. A device that I have borrowed from psychodrama and, sometimes, used effectively is described below:

Carmen, a young Argentinian woman, married to an American, had returned to Argentina for a visit. While in her native country, she had run into a man she had been in love with several years before meeting her husband. Back in the United States, Carmen, who loved and had an excellent relationship with her husband, was troubled and disturbed by the fact that many nostalgic memories had been aroused by that chance encounter with her old flame. Upon receiving Carmen's communication, the group remained silent for several minutes, after which I made the following statement "We probably have, all of us, old relationships in our past and, once in a while memories of them intrude in our present. As Carmen was talking, I had an intuition that what she said brought some of these memories back. Could we take turns and go into a brief monologue, as if we were talking to ouselves and state our thoughts out loud, or 'pass' as the case may be." Without exception, all group members talked about past relationships they were thinking about. When they were done, Carmen reached for the two group members on each side of her and said "Thank you, that is just what I needed to know, thank you."

One more point must be made. Sensing the mood of the group and grasping the true meaning of an interaction requires that the therapist be truly part of the group and transcend the observer's role, always keeping in mind that the needs of the group members have always precedence over the needs of the therapist. The therapist must be able to experience, not just infer from observations, the group's anxieties, desires, joys, sorrows, currents, and undercurrents.

FOCUSING ON THE GROUP'S BEHAVIOR.   It is, of course, apparent that the group leader's behaviors described so far overlap and cannot be discreetly categorized except for descriptive and explanatory purposes. The therapist is supportive, while being a model and, at the same time, enhancing an effective process. This is particularly true of the therapist's interventions in helping the group or persons within the group to focus on their own behavior. Indeed, when a person or a group focuses on their own behavior, they become aware of the fact that they may have strayed from the "here-and-now." Yet, the concept of "focusing on one's behavior" is somewhat more encompassing hence its discussion under a separate heading. For example, even when the group is in the "here-and-now," and avoidance is not present, focusing on the behavior as it occurs may intensify feelings, clarify the communications exchanged, and provide insight into the avoidance mechanisms used as well as insight into one's inability to convey a communication. This will be illustrated in the following examples.

This particular incident was already referred to at the beginning of this section. Group members had come in agitated and troubled because of two unsolved murders in our community. Two group members, Mary-Joe and Tom, had engaged into a seemingly irrelevant argument about men and women while the rest of the group remained silent. After several minutes, the following interaction took place:

Therapist: Let us stop for a minute. What do you see happening right now?
Joe: Who the hell cares about all this?
Nancy: I am scared. I am even scared to talk about what I am scared about.
Joe: I am angry also. I'm really mad. I wish I could lay my hands on the guy who did that and tear him apart.
Therapist: Yet, we were not sharing these feelings.
Nancy: I guess it was easier to let Mary-Joe and Tom do it in a nutty way, but ... I tell you ... I am scared.

This was Joanne's initial session and, at the end of the meeting, she related briefly the recent death of her husband as a result of a freak accident. The group started the next meeting a week later with much spontaneous and pleasant levity. The light exchanges, however, dragged on indefinitely. As this time went on, I commented "This was very pleasant, yet I wonder whether we are not, perhaps, using this light conversation to avoid something." The group said nothing but Joanne talked about the loneliness of her life as a widow. Death and separation were discussed and the group left with a feeling of warmth and closeness.

In the first example, feelings of fear and anger were expressed through the medium of two group members and in an indirect and disguised manner. In the second example, feelings of loneliness and fears of death and separation were being avoided. The therapist's interventions by momentarily freezing the action and focusing on what was happening helped the group become involved, in touch with their feelings and back in the "here-and-now."

There are times when the pace of the exchanges is too fast to be interrupted. In such cases it may be more advisable for the therapist not to freeze the action but to allow it to unravel until there is a lull in the process.

> Barbara was an open and honest but moralistic and self-right-eous woman in her late forties. Rhea, 25-years-old, was rebel-lious, assertive, and occasionally intolerant. They constantly irritated each other and on that particular evening were engaged into a rather violent confrontation. The following exchanges took place:
>
> Barbara: I think you are a brat and, if you were my daughter, you would have toed the line, don't you think so, Grace?
> Grace (a teacher): I try to make my children listen, but I don't want to stifle them.
> Barbara: I don't want to stifle my kids either, but I think they should mind their elders.
> Rhea: Bullshit.
> Bill: That's the problem with modern educational methods. You don't know what to do.
> Sondra (jokingly): It's all Dr. Spock's fault. (A brief silence ensued).
> Therapist: Would you be willing to go back in time and look at the past three minutes as through a microscope. What do you think has happened?
>
> The group was willing to "go back in time," picked on the confrontation, on Barbara's vain effort to enlist Grace's help, traced the manner in which the group had left the "here-and-now" through a discussion on educational methods and became aware of how angry feelings were defused through a joke.

THE INDIVIDUAL, THE DYAD, OR THE GROUP?   The question some-times arises as to whether the leader's intervention should focus on the individual, the dyad, or the group as a whole. It must be made clear that the kind of intervention discussed here still has to do with the process (i.e., the manner in which the communication is conveyed) and not with the content (i.e., the communication itself). There is, of course, no definite answer and, in order to make his or her decision, the leader must be tuned in to what constitutes the foreground and background of the action and how and when foreground and background alternate. These terms, borrowed from Gestalt psychology and adapted to the group therapy situation, should be explained briefly. When a person conveys a communication or two people within a group communicate with each other, some covert communication emanates also from the group at the same time. Vice versa, when a group as a whole discusses an issue of common interest, persons within the group may, most often without being aware of it, send their own messages. The overt message, the one on which attention is focused, is the foreground; the covert, sometimes unconscious message, is the background. The following examples will illustrate the above concepts:

> The group was engrossed in the discussion of a group member's pending marriage, sharing with each other their experiences, memories, etc. While these exchanges were going on, Barbara was silent and looked very somber. The group discussion was the foreground; Barbara's behavior was background. When a group member turned to Barbara and asked her whether there was something the matter with her, Barbara's behavior became foreground and the group's behavior became background.

If the ongoing process in the foreground is effective and a background process is muddled, the leader will allow the foreground process to terminate and then will deal with the less effective background process thus bringing it into the foreground (unless, of course, someone else in the group intervenes as was the case in the preceding example). If the foreground process is not effective, then the leader may choose to deal with it and, if necessary, ignore the background covert process or deal with it at a later time. This is again illustrated in the following anecdotes:

> This particular incident has already been mentioned at the beginning of this section. Paulette had announced her termination from group and Frank had attacked her and her decision to leave. Somewhat impatiently, the group listened to the exchange and, after a while, Tom, another group member, stated "What's the matter with you, Frank? You sound like you are spoiling for a fight." When the inappropriateness of Frank's behavior was pointed out to him, he accepted the feedback but insisted on the genuineness of his feelings and requested the group's help in understanding them. After much give and take, sometimes moving, sometimes amusing, Frank acknowledged mixed feelings toward Paulette, feelings of intense affection and feelings of resentment because she had never seemed impressed with his rugged masculinity. Above all, he acknowledged that he would miss her very much. Frank and Paulette embraced, the group went on to another topic and, for a few minutes, Frank and Paulette remained close to each other, their hands around each other's shoulders.

Initially, the interaction between Frank and Paulette was the foreground, and the group's irritation at Frank was the background. The leader could have pointed out the inappropriateness of Frank's comments or could have focused on the group's irritation. None of these interventions proved necessary because the group dealt with the situation. The group's behavior (discussion of Frank's feelings) then became the foreground and, of course, no intervention was necessary. Later, as the group went on to something else, Frank's and Paulette's nonverbal exchange of affection was the background and, again, no intervention was called for.

> The group, in a state of flux during several weeks with the accompanying anxiety, had been joined by two new members. Relief at what was perceived to be a consolidation of a shaky group was mingled with the excitement and anxiety of the new members. There was a lot of joking, almost silly levity for a while, until the group, with some prodding by the group leader,

began dealing with the relief they had experienced at seeing new members (i.e., it had been the group's consensus that unless new members joined within three weeks the group would disband). Judith, during the first 15 minutes of the session, looked sad and withdrawn without saying anything. Later, however, she joined into the group's levity.

The foreground, at the beginning of the session, was the group's joking and silliness. The process was not very effective in that the message (e.g., relief and anxiety) was not expressed clearly. The background was Judith's sad feelings relatively well-conveyed through her posture and facial expression. The therapist chose to deal first with the ineffective group process. The therapist could have faced the decision of whether to go back then and pick on Judith's nonverbal behavior and bring it to the foreground or ignore it until such time as Judith chose to convey again that same communication. In that particular session, however, this did not become necessary because, later during the meeting, Judith chose to verbally share her problem with the group.

REFLECTING FEELINGS.   Conveying a communication at all levels, verbal as well as nonverbal, intellectual as well as emotional, is not easy; hearing that communication at all levels, what is said as well as what is felt, can be even more difficult. Often, a group member, having surmounted his or her fears, tries to communicate openly and honestly and yet feels unheard. Sometimes, he or she is not heard because of an inability to communicate and, at other times, because group members have not yet learned to hear. Whatever the reason, to feel unheard, especially when one makes an effort at communicating, can be painful and discouraging. A simple reflection of feelings on the part of the therapist may be sufficient to make the group member feel that he or she is being heard and encourage him or her to continue the process of self-exploration and interpersonal communication. Reflecting feelings is used here strictly within a client-centered context (Rogers, 1951). Describing or dwelling on it any further would be redundant. A note of caution, however, may be necessary. Very quickly, group members learn to hear. They are even quicker to learn that they care and to try to hear each other. The group leader must be careful not to upstage group members and make him-or herself the center of the action.

LECTURETTES. The therapist's interventions should not be limited by established rules and theoretical considerations except as such rules and considerations pertain to the preservation of group member's dignity, respect, and welfare. Outside of these parameters therapists can innovate and experiment. A technique that I have called *lecturette* was prompted by the realization that, while involved with and very much a part of my groups, I maintain more objectivity than group members. This objectivity is recognized and accepted by group members and enables me on rare occasions to pontificate selectively and moderately as in the following example.

> At the beginning of the session, one of the group members shared with us the recent death of his mother. He was very sad and cried and much support and sympathy were directed at him. A long silence followed. I wondered if perhaps we were all thinking of loved ones who had died or whose death was pending. Indeed, that was the case and much sorrow and fear were shared. The mood was definitely depressed and somber. I made, then, the following statement: "There are deaths and there are births, sorrows and joys. Have you seen the picture *Zorba the Greek?* After a beautiful woman is killed, Zorba is angered at the inevitability of death and the musical score, at that very moment, is so sad that it tears one's heart apart. The single notes on the bouzouki are like tears falling one by one. Then Zorba's friend says "Teach me to dance, will you?" and, as Zorba replies "Did you say dance? Come, my boy!" the music changes. It becomes like a dawn, like fireworks, like a joyous hymn to life and rebirth. I would like you to hear it." Without waiting for an answer I played the tape of Theodorakis' music, and, as it changed and the tempo picked up, we all spontaneously stood, held each other and started to dance. Death was transformed and, even John, whose mother had died, joined with us in the celebration of life.

That session stood as one of the most memorable in the history of that particular group.

NONVERBAL COMMUNICATIONS.   Nonverbal communications are important and almost always genuine and revealing. When the nonverbal message is congruent with its verbal counterpart, no intervention is, of course, called for. When nonverbal and verbal messages, however, are at odds, it may be advisable for the therapist to help the group or the individual focus on that discrepancy. Needless to say, caution is again necessary. Nonverbal language is complex and to decipher or interpret it is difficult and better not be attempted unless one is fairly positive of the meaning of the message. Interpretations of nonverbal messages can often be incorrect and, even when correct, may be rejected by the person. It is often sufficient to point out the discrepancy and let the group or the individual do what they want with that knowledge. Some examples follow.

> Therapist to group: Usually we sit close to each other. Today, there seems to be so much space between us.
> Therapist to group member: I get the uncomfortable feeling that, at times, you send mixed messages. You said something very sad but you prefaced your comments with a smile.
> Therapist to group member: I am curious. You are leaning forward as if you want to say something. Yet, you cover your mouth with your hands.

Such comments should not be overused. Obviously, if the nonverbal and the verbal communication are not congruent it is because at some level the person does not wish to convey the nonverbal message. Continually focusing attention on what one does not wish to reveal makes a person vulnerable and robs him or her of spontaneity.

INTERPRETATIONS AND GROUP PROCESS.   Most of the interventions described above, designed to render the process more effective, have one feature in common. They render the members of the group aware of the ineffectiveness of the ongoing process and allow them to draw their own conclusions. While this approach is fruitful, a case can be made for more involved interventions including interpretations of the process by the therapist. The controversy is, I believe, rather important and, instead of being dealt with in this section, will be considered a clinical issue and treated in greater length in Chapter 6.

DEALING WITH THE CONTENT

Finally, the last major category of the leader's behavior is helping group members deal with the content of their communication. Indeed, it was stated at the beginning of this book that two classes of events occur in a group. People talk and relate to each other (i.e., process), and they talk about specific things (i.e., content). Very often the content of their communication has to do with expressions of feelings, feedback, and confrontation. In other words, it is limited to "here-and-now" interactions among group members. At other times, however, the content of the communication is problems experienced by group members either in their everyday life or in their past but affecting their present. As is the case in individual psychotherapy, members of a therapy group can and should be helped to deal with such problems.

Very often, the help and solutions are provided through the group's interactions. For example, all Carmen (the Argentinian woman mentioned earlier in this chapter) wanted and needed was the reassurance that other people could also be rendered nostalgic by past relationships. John, the young man whose mother had died, had his sorrow relieved through the group's shared feelings.

The group can also help in a more complex manner and for less clearcut problems. Earlier in this chapter, an interaction was described between Barbara, a moralistic and self-righteous woman in her forties and Rhea, a rebellious, assertive, sometimes hostile 25-year-old. During the latter part of the session, the group, with much intuitiveness and sensitivity, helped Rhea trace much of her hostility to a relationship with a rejecting and demanding mother as well as work those feelings through.

On the other hand, there are times when the group cannot help. The reader will remember the interaction between Paulette and Frank. Frank was helped to put his inappropriate feelings in proper perspective and got in touch with his positive feelings toward Paulette. The group had done nothing to help Frank with the past experiences that had distorted his relationships with women. In such instances, when the group's help comes to a halt, the therapist may intervene, as in individual therapy. The kind of intervention will vary with the nature of the problem, the therapist's training, preference, and theoretical orientation. Any approach is legitimate provided, of course, that the rights and dignity of the individual be preserved and that the therapist be well trained in the theory and practice of the approach used. My preference is to use psychodrama as developed by J. L. Moreno. The reasons for my preference, the basic elements of psychodrama, as well as appropriate illustrations, will be delineated in an addendum at the end of the book.

Reviewing my notes on the hundreds of group sessions that I have led over the past 13 years, I became aware that, by no means, have I exhausted the possible categories of interventions available to a leader. I have selected those that were more apparent to me and with which I felt more comfortable. As stated at the beginning of this chapter, the group therapist, within certain parameters, must feel free to innovate and experiment.

The reader may mistakenly perceive, from this chapter, that the group leader must intervene constantly. This false impression may have been derived from the fact that I had to focus upon the leader's behavior. While I do not believe that a group leader is allowed to shirk his or her responsibilities (nor do I believe in the "great stone face" syndrome with which many therapists are afflicted), I do believe in the wisdom of the group and, therefore, I make my interventions as scarce as possible. Eventually, as a group learns to communicate, the therapist's interventions are no longer needed.

SUMMARY

The tasks of the leader can be conceptualized as divided into four major categories. Each category is, then, defined, by its subdivisions as follows:

I.   *The leader must promote a climate of trust, support, and mutual respect.*
1.   The leader should avoid verbal and/or nonverbal behaviors tending to belittle, ridicule, or humiliate group members.
2.   The leader should avoid implied, subtle, or overt rejection of group members who choose to remain defensive and uninvolved. The leader should recognize that people move at different paces.
3.   The leader should avoid applying pressure upon group members to conform to his or her standards.
4.   Under certain circumstances, the leader should encourage appropriate physical expressions of support.
II.   *The group leader must offer himself or herself as a model.*
1.   The leader must be aware of and comfortable with his or her feelings.
2.   The leader must be able to express his or her feelings appropriately.
   a.   Initially, the therapist should express his or her feelings honestly but gradually.
   b.   The therapist's angry and affectionate feelings toward group members should be expressed with caution.

3. The leader may discuss his or her own problems only when appropriate and under certain conditions.

III. *The group leader may resort to certain interventions in order to enhance communication and hasten an effective process.*

1. Factor slowing down an "effective process."
   a. The communicator, be it the group as a whole or the individual within the group may not be aware of what they wish to convey or of ineffectiveness in the process.
   b. The "ineffective process" may be used as a defense.
   c. The communicator may have forgotten how or may have never learned to convey a communication effectively.

2. Possible interventions.
   a. Returning to the "here-and-now."
   b. Focusing on the group's behavior.
   c. Should one focus on the individual, the dyad, or the group?
   d. Reflecting feelings.
   e. Lecturettes.
   f. Bringing attention to the use of nonverbal communications.
   g. Interpretations and group process.

IV. *Dealing with the content of the communication.*

Chapter 5

LOGISTICS AND CLINICAL ISSUES

In the preceding chapter, the tasks of the leader were described and discussed from a generic point of view. Promoting a climate of trust, offering oneself as a model, enhancing communication, and so on, enter to a greater or less extent into almost all of the leader's behavior. Within that encompassing umbrella are additional group leaders' responsibilities and specific behaviors that have not been rendered justice in the preceding chapter but that bear discussion. For purposes of classification, I have divided these responsibilities and behaviors into two categories that I have titled *Logistics and Clinical Issues.*

LOGISTICS

Group therapy, like all forms of therapy, is a transaction. The therapist sells a commodity that is purchased directly by the client or indirectly by the client's representative, for example, the sources that fund the clinics or institutions offering the therapy. As in all honorable business transactions, the buyer must be aware of what he or she is buying and of exactly what he or she is expected to pay in exchange. These are termed the *logistics* of group therapy and will be discussed below. There is one difference, however, between therapy and other kinds of business transactions. Unlike other business situations, it is incumbent upon the therapist to insure as much as possible that the client will benefit from the services that are purchased. Hence, the therapist has a duty to interview and, if necessary, refuse to accept group members who could, perhaps not be helped or be hurt (or even hurt other group members) by the group process. For this reason, the topic of interviewing and selecting members will be discussed in this section.

Interviewing and Choosing Members

Citing appropriate references, Yalom states that there is much clinical concensus that patients who are brain damaged, paranoid, extremely narcissistic, hypochondriacal, suicidal, addicted, acutely psychotic, or sociopathic are poor candidates for outpatient intensive group therapy (Yalom, 1978). In the same chapter, Yalom suggests criteria for identification of clients who may drop out of therapy prematurely. While these criteria are, indeed, useful they are not, of course, infallible. Patients who are subject to external stresses or display the character traits cited by Yalom as reasons for failing in group therapy may, indeed, do well with one therapist and fail with another. I will, therefore, suggest an alternate mode of selecting patients for groups. Instead of studying the patient to determine whether that particular patient will do well in group, I suggest that the therapist study him- or herself to become aware of the type of patient to whom he or she does not resonate or feel uncomfortable with.

The initial step in this process is to overcome two of the most prevalent and cherished beliefs among inexperienced (and, sometimes, experienced) therapists. The first such belief is that patients drop out of or fail to improve in therapy because they are "bad" patients or poor candidates for a specific treatment modality.

The second is that a good therapist should be able to accept, feel comfortable with, and deal with all kinds of patients. The next step is to honestly come to grips with oneself, recognize that there are clients with whom some of us are not successful but who could be helped by others; this next step is to become aware of our fears, biases, anxieties, prejudices, and how they may interfere with our interpersonal relationships, especially with our clients. The odds are excellent that if a sample of therapists were to be asked the type of clients they would not wish to have in their groups, their list would duplicate that of Yalom as cited above. The point is, however, that not all therapists would be allergic to all of the above categories of patients. Rather than a blank indictment of all these categories, group leaders could be discriminating, accepting some "poor candidates" with whom they feel more comfortable and rejecting those to whom they definitely feel unable to relate. The following remarks gleaned from a recorded discussion of therapists in training illustrates the point.*

> "I can't stand the silent type. That's the one who really gets me; makes me feel like a damn failure."
>
> "The silent characters don't bother me; after a while, I pay no attention to them."
>
> "Mentally retarded make me feel very uncomfortable, almost guilty."
>
> "I like to work with mentally retarded; there is something gentle, almost doe-like about them which appeals to me."
>
> "There was one who played therapist all the time and always wanted to take over the group. I know that my

*I wish to thank my students of the October, 1977–August 1978 class for their very helpful contributions to this discussion.

own insecurity entered a lot into it but I was damn glad when he dropped out."

"The angry, hostile type I would think twice before accepting in the group."

"I welcome a hostile group member. I feel I can stand up to him and it has a good effect on the group."

In addition to becoming aware of their fears, likes and dislikes, biases and preferences, therapists must ask themselves another related question. What is their level of stress tolerance? How much is a therapist willing to take? Obviously, many patients, even when not belonging to any of the above categories, can be difficult, taxing the patience, the stamina and the good will of the therapist. There is nothing that says that a therapist should have unlimited patience or subject him- or herself to undue stress. It is essential, however, that the therapist be aware of his or her stress threshold and abide by it, for example, refuse patients who would push the level of stress beyond that particular therapists's threshold. As already stated earlier, it is quite true that some patients are taxing and difficult to deal with. Labeling them "poor candidates," however, implies that they will do poorly with all therapists. Using as a criterion the therapist's own level of stress tolerance suggests that the "poor" candidate may be a "good" candidate with another therapist with a higher stress threshold.

Finally, in selecting members for a new group or new members for an already ongoing group, the group leader must be aware of the amount of faith he or she has in the group, the extent to which he or she tends to take over and feel responsible, and the extent to which he or she allows the group to develop and take care of its own affairs. The greater the therapist's confidence in the group and the lesser his or her belief in his or her omnipotence, the more flexible and tolerant he or she will be in accepting and selecting members.

Other additional factors, of course, enter into play such as the configuration of the group, the length of time a group has been together, etc. There are, however, neither rules nor experimental data dictating which categories of people work well together in a group. The group therapist will be guided by his or her experiences, common sense and preferences, and his or her predictions will improve as experience increases with time.

When the therapist chooses a new member for an ongoing group rather than selecting members in order to form a new group, one more important factor has to be taken into consideration: the opinion of the group members already in the group. Introducing new members affects the nature of the group as well as, possibly, the status of old members in the group. As always, members must have a choice in the process of introducing new people. On the other hand, it is unrealistic to give group members veto power over adding new members. In private practice, maintaining the level of members provides constancy to the therapist's income; in institutional work, there is usually a waiting list for clients wishing to enter a group. A veto power on the addition of new group members would allow the clients to manipulate the therapist's income or the destiny of people whom they have never seen. It would be unfeasible to allow group members to interview and then accept or reject new applicants. Such procedures could be destructive to the rejected applicant. It would also violate their confidentiality in the sense that, if rejected, much will be known about them by members of a group to which they will not belong.

To maintain control upon my income and to prevent rejection of potential group members in need of help, while at the same time granting to members of the ongoing group a say in what happens in the group, I build the following clauses into the contract.

1. No group will have more than ten members except in some extraordinary circumstance and only by consensus.
2. Whenever a group member terminates, a new member will automatically take his or her place.

3. The group leader will consult with the group regarding the timing of a new member's introduction. If it is the members' consensus that the group is going through a critical phase or that some important issues are being worked through, the introduction of the new member will be delayed for as long as necessary.

In addition to the above formal rules and without identifying the prospective new members, I briefly discuss them with the group as a matter of courtesy. Never have I encountered an unambiguous negative reaction, and mixed feelings have the opportunity to be worked through, at least to some extent, before the new member joins the group.

A question that often arises in connection with choosing group members is to what extent does the therapist know the new applicant. There is really no adequate answer and therapists will end up doing what they feel most comfortable with.* Some therapists require several months of individual therapy before considering a new member. Others are satisfied with one interview only. The majority of my group members have been in individual therapy with me before joining a group. I do not, however, consider a period of individual therapy as a requirement for acceptance to a group. As a matter of fact, many of my group members are accepted or rejected after one interview only. Indeed, while I can hardly diagnose or assess an applicant within one session, I can tell whether I feel comfortable with and can relate to him or her. Since this is my main criterion for acceptance, I find that one interview is sufficient. I also believe that to see an applicant a number of times before making a decision presents certain disadvantages for the potential new member. Expectations are built in the prospective new applicant and a relationship begins to be established, if not on the

*I am indebted to my colleagues of the Group Therapy Clinic of the Western Psychiatric Institute and Clinic (WPIC) Pittsburgh for an illuminating discussion of this topic.

part of the therapist, certainly on the part of the client. Rejection, after a series of meetings, may be experienced as a sense of failure and generate anxiety and other negative reactions.

The Contract

Earlier in this chapter the word *transaction* was used to describe individual as well as group therapy. In the preceding section, the emphasis was placed upon the group leader's criteria for selecting applicants. Joining a group, however, is a two-way street and, although each prospective group member has his or her own criteria for joining, it is important that as much and as accurate information as possible be available before the decision is made. The prospective group member must be aware of what he or she is getting into *before* joining, aware of the leader's obligations, as well as of the member's obligations.

THE GROUP LEADER'S OBLIGATIONS

A Description of the Process.   When interviewing new applicants, I go to great lengths in explaining what therapy means to me, what happens in the group, and why it happens. I describe briefly what happens in a psychodrama because I use that modality quite extensively in order to deal with content. Without being unrealistic and raising false expectations, I explain why and how a group experience may be of help to the candidate's specific problems. There have been times when a candidate, as a result of my explanations, changed his or her mind and instead opted for individual or family therapy. I also describe in vague and very general terms the people who are already in the group (if the candidate is assessed for placement into an already ongoing group). I encourage questions and answer them as honestly as I can. I make no particular effort to alleviate the candidate's anxiety because I believe that the anxiety in dealing with an opening up to people should be dealt with within the context of the group.

The Therapist's Presence and an Adequate Meeting Place.   In addition to his or her skills and competence, the therapist sells and is paid for his or her time. Being present during the time for which the clients have contracted is simply honest business practice. I do my best to be always on time and, when late, I make the time up. There are times when, for a variety of reasons, such as catching a plane to go to a convention, I cannot keep the group for the full 2 hours (i.e., the length of my sessions). In such instances, I notify the group ahead of time and we make arrangements for a longer session at another time. On the other hand, when a group meets in the evening or at the end of a working day and no other client or clients are expected at my office, I allow the group to run longer than the 2 hours contracted for. There have been times when the group has gone on for as long as 3 or 3½ hours. I do not know whether or not this is sound clinical practice, however, I have noticed that longer sessions have always been beneficial and never did I feel manipulated by my clients. Instead, they were always grateful for the extra time.

It is also important that the therapist provide an adequate and comfortable meeting place. The room where my groups meet (affectionately called the "group room") is adjacent to my main office. It is accessible through the main office as well as through the hallway. Group members who come in early do not have to wait in the waiting room but may enter the group room directly. This is convenient for college students or people employed who do not have time to go home for dinner between the end of the working day and the time at which group begins. Often, together with a sandwich and a book, the group room becomes a haven for a short while. The group room is fairly large. One half of it is used for the group and easily accommodates ten people; the other half, with four director's chairs and a system of colored lights is used for psychodrama. Large-sized pillows are on the floor although group members who so prefer may use chairs. This happens infrequently, almost exclusively when a member suffers from a backache. I favor pillows because

I believe that chairs, especially easy, comfortable chairs can be islands of safety within themselves from which people can be reluctant to move. I found that pillows lend a certain fluidity and group members too inhibited to leave their chairs and move toward someone else find it much easier to slide their pillows close to a person they wish to comfort and support. The room is painted a pleasant yellow and, except for a serape that I brought in from Mexico, is decorated with contributions from group members who have been long gone.

The Group Leader's Total Involvement. The group leader should devote his or her total involvement to the group. Whether or not this is always possible is another matter. Transitory events, fatigue, and occasional stress will, of course, interfere with the therapist's involvement and concentration. Such conditions, however, should not be allowed to persist. If the therapist's personal life causes such chronic stress that it interferes with his or her listening and concentrating, then it is incumbent upon the therapist to remedy the situation by seeking personal help elsewhere.

Availability and Confidentiality. The therapist's responsibility does not end when the two hours are up. In the process of reacquiring awareness and putting a closure to unfinished business, group sessions may reopen old wounds and reawaken old sorrows. Sometimes, it takes quite a while for the dust to settle, and in between sessions, group members may experience severe stress. It is reassuring to know that there is someone that one can turn to if need be. While I strongly encourage the members of my groups to bring their conflicts, unexpected and sudden fears, or depression to the group rather than talk to me, I am available at all times for emergencies. Over the past eleven years, I was called very rarely and almost always literally for matters of life and death when a patient was contemplating suicide. The few times group members called me for topics that were not of an emergency nature, I could always convince them to wait until the group met and the group's response was so supportive that these members seldom called me again. I found that for many of my group members the knowledge of my availability was what mattered.

Treating what is said by group members as privileged communication is such an obvious obligation of the leader that it should not even be discussed. In recent years, however, so many different kinds of groups have proliferated, so many have been conducted publicly or under the glare of television lights that it is easy for a beginning therapist to forget that, unless clearly specified otherwise in the contract, group members are entitled to exactly the same confidentiality as individual patients.

THE MEMBER'S OBLIGATIONS.   There are two sides to any transaction and the client as well as the therapist must fulfill certain obligations. These obligations, however, must be made very clear. The client must understand them thoroughly and truly have the choice to accept them or reject them. I lump these obligations together under the heading of "rules." I explain them clearly and make certain that they are throughly understood and accepted before the clients join the group. These "rules" may be described as follows.

Confidentiality.   Some group leaders, especially within the encounter movement feel that, by joining a group, the individual implicitly accepts the possibility that confidentiality may, and probably will, not be kept and, therefore, the group leader may not request that confidentiality be a condition for acceptance. While there is some truth to the fact that confidentiality cannot be guaranteed, it is my belief that group members are entitled to some consensual agreement that what they choose to reveal will not be discussed outside of the group. I demand, therefore, of all members that they abide by the principle of confidentiality and consider what is said in group as privileged communication.

Attendance.   I explain to a prospective member that groups tend to become cohesive, and that a group member's absence or tardiness may be damaging to the group. For example, a group member may wish to discuss an important matter but decides against doing so because of the absence of another group member on whose support and understanding he or she counted on. To arrive on time and to attend sessions regularly are one of the group's rules.

Freedom.   This rule, called freedom for want of a better word is somewhat more difficult to define. I explain that, having been accepted into a group, the new member is free to proceed at his or her own speed and is not under the obligation to perform, conform, or abide by any norms that may initially be distasteful or frightening. I point out, however, that "freedom" works both ways and that the other members are also free to prod a group member who chooses to remain an observer rather than a participant.

Socializing Outside of Group Sessions.   I request that, should a close relationship develop between two group members outside of the group, the other members be appraised of that fact. I explain that innuendo or nonverbal communications, between two people who know each other may well confuse the rest of the group and thus impede communication unless the group is made aware of that relationship. The appropriateness of socializing outside of the group setting is a matter of controversy and will be discussed later in this chapter.

Payment of Fees.   After stating my fees and my request that my statement presented at the end of each month, be paid within 30 days, I am also very specific in explaining a clause in the contract. According to that clause, *group members are liable for the fee whether or not they attend the session.* I justify insertion of that clause in the contract by explaining that my time is committed to the group members and should be accordingly remunerated, even if one group member decides on a whim not to attend; and the knowledge that they would be charged anyway limits unnecessary absences to a minimum. I keep my fees slightly lower than the prevailing group fees in our area to make up for the times group members are charged for unavoidable absences. Since Community Mental Health Centers have become operational, I have discontinued granting reductions in fees. On the other hand, if the financial situation of a client changes abruptly for reasons beyond his or her control such as the loss of a job or catastrophic illness to a family member, I continue to see him or her in the group for as long as necessary at a reduced fee or at no fee. The fact is never made known by me to the other group members. There have been instances, however, when the group member chose to share this information with the rest of the group.

CLINICAL ISSUES

For want of a better term, I have titled the leader's responsibilities and behaviors discussed below *clinical issues.* The list is, by no means, exhaustive. The issues that I will describe are those with which I have been most often confronted. I am sure that each therapist will eventually have to come to grips with situations that either have been discussed elsewhere or not been discussed at all. At such times, the therapist will have to rely upon his or her care for the group members, common sense, and intuition.

Interpretation Versus Acknowledging the Process

Toward the end of the preceding chapter, it was pointed out that most of the leader's interventions already described were designed to make the group members aware of the ineffectiveness of the ongoing process and to allow them to draw their own conclusions. They stopped short of being interpretative. For example, they offered no explanations for the ineffective process. This is not to say that more involved interventions on the part of the therapist, including interpretations of the process, are not very legitimate and often quite fruitful. In endless discussions with other group therapists, I have become aware that many distinguished colleagues favor such interpretaions. It is, by now, clear to the reader that my preference is to use interpretations very parsimoniously, if at all, and I would like to build a case for my approach while encouraging the reader and prospective group therapists to experiment with various approaches and settle for the one with which they feel more comfortable.

As repeatedly stated throughout this book, an ineffective process serves defensive purposes. Sometimes, it has become habitual and the communicator is not aware that the garbled communication served, at one time, as a protection. At other times, the communicator is aware that he or she is holding back and not conveying a clear and complete message and yet chooses to do so. In the first case, interpretations may be appropriate, helpful, and welcome. In the second case, simply pointing out that the communication is ineffective may be enough; an interpretation may be threatening to a person who feels vulnerable and experiences the need for a defensive tactic. It must be remembered that a group leader should be finely tuned in and very intuitive in order to perceive the difference between the two instances. Such intuitiveness and perceptivity may not always be possible. In the first instance, for example, when the ineffective process has become a habit and the communicator is not aware that he or she is not communicating clearly, an interpretation may hasten the advent of a more effective process. Abstaining from providing an interpretation may slow the effective process but will cause no damage. In the second instance, for example, when the communicator is aware that he or she is not communicating clearly, an untimely interpretation may be damaging. If I have to err, then I prefer to err on the side of my client's safety and abstain as much as possible from making interpretations that may be harmful.

The group leader who favors interpretations is faced with additional questions. "Are the interpretations correct? Are they timely?" If the interpretation is incorrect, and especially if the therapist is trusted and liked, then the clients may believe that interpretation and their perceptions of themselves and of the ongoing process will become distorted as a result of accepting an incorrect interpretation of what is happening. If the interpretation is correct but untimely, then the situation alluded to in the preceeding paragraph will occur. The client (or group) may reject the interpretation in anger or accept it and be hurt, even devastated. Again, I prefer to abstain and to simply point out the process. An alternative that I favor, when appropriate and possible, is to acknowledge the process and at the same time share my own feelings about what is happening. More often than not, my feelings will reflect the feelings of the group, help group members become more in touch with what they are experiencing and even, perhaps, gain insight into the reasons underlying the manner in which they have related. The following examples will illustrate some of the concepts described above. These examples could have just as well been included in the preceding chapter in the section on enhancing communication and hastening an effective process. I have chosen to include them in this section because they focus on alternatives to interpretations but I wish to emphasize that all the suggested alternatives tend toward a common goal: better communication.

Deborah was a very attractive woman in her early thirties. Gentle, friendly, she perpetually displayed a smile and a happy face no matter what the circumstances might be. The smile eventually began to irritate the other group members who confronted her with their irritation but to no avail. Deborah would simply say "You are right" or "What's wrong with smiling" and would keep on smiling. One evening, Deborah was relating to us a particularly bitter fight she had had with her husband and was chuckling while talking. There was something poignant about her chuckle and I made the following comment. "I have an image in my mind of a neat little girl, with a very clean dress and well combed hair who would like very much to cry but cannot because she knows her parents always want her to look happy even when she isn't." For the first time, Deborah's face became serious, somewhat pensive. She stopped talking about the fight with her husband and said "I like that little girl, I feel I know her ... I think I must be like her but I don't even know when I smile ..." This was the beginning of Deborah's coming to grips with her real feelings and, when a year later she left the group, she smiled much less but more genuinely. Deborah was an example of a person who was not aware of the garbled message which she conveyed and the interpretation was accepted and proved helpful.

Leroy was an intelligent, sensitive, black graduate student in an all-white group composed of four female and one other male member. Leroy was open with his feelings, yet he had never been angry in the group or expressed negative comments toward anyone. As the group members were marveling at his good nature, one of the co-leaders (the group was co-led by an experienced therapist and a young student) stated "Leroy is extra nice because we are all white and he is afraid if he antagonizes us he will be rejected." Leroy's eyes filled with tears and he said nothing. During the next few sessions he remained silent and withdrawn. He would probably have been able to work through his conflict in the group but unfortunately his father, an industrial engineer, was transferred to another city. Leroy's last session with the group was strained and painful. One of his last comments was to the effect that he did not think he would join a group again.

The above anecdote illustrates what may happen when interpretations, while correct, are verbalized at the wrong time and without the support that helps render them less threatening. The following anecdotes illustrate situations affording more than one alternative to the leader.

Due to leave for one week's vacation, I suggested that the group might want to meet without me on that week. A group member states "Yes, I think we can do that. I am sure that we can help each other." After a while, a second group member added "But we shall miss you." At that moment, a number of alternatives that I could have said (in addition, of course, to that of saying nothing at all) were available to me as follows:
"What I am hearing you say is that you can hack it without me, but at the same time, you don't want to hurt my feelings. Who knows? I may get angry and retaliate."

"You can hack it without me but you really don't want to hurt my feelings by telling me so."

"It is exciting but also somewhat scary to do it by oneself. Is that what you are trying to say?"

"You can hack it by yourselves but you are concerned about my feelings. And, I guess I do have mixed feelings about it. Part of me is very happy that you can do it alone. Part of me is a little afraid, a little bit hurt, but also feels good at your concern."

Which of the above answers is preferable? They are, I believe, all quite acceptable, and to some extent, reflect the therapist's concerns and personality. For example, a therapist concerned with the possibility that he or she is hostile may be tuned in to negative reactions and favor the first answer. On the other hand, a therapist who tends to be supportive will prefer answer number two. Both answers have some interpretative elements in them. The third alternative is less interpretative and focuses somewhat more sharply on the feelings of the group and the dependence/independence conflict. Caution, however, should be exercised in phrasing it as, in this particular example, the line differentiating an intellectual interpretation from a reflection of feelings is quite thin. Whereas a reflection of feelings could be acceptable, an intellectual interpretation could have less impact. I personally favor the fourth alternative that accomplishes a number of things simultaneously. It acknowledges the process and enables me to share my own feelings with the group. In addition, it points out the dependence/independence conflict from the therapist's point of view.

The group was composed of five women and four men and on that particular evening all men happened to be absent. The women present chose to talk about disappointments experienced in heterosexual relationships, for example, rejection by boyfriends and/or husbands, divorces, etc. Until then, the group had only skirted that topic. It was quite conceivable that the group's configuration, for example, the absence of men, for some reason enabled the women to discuss in depth what was an important conflict in their lives. What were some of the alternatives available to the leader?

1. The first alternative would be to say nothing and allow the discussion to proceed.

2. Another alternative would be to trace what was happening to the absence of the men in the group.

3. To help the group become aware that the absence of men on that day triggered old feelings of rejection, loneliness, and missed relationships.

The second alternative, for example, to point out that the group's configuration was different would be technically correct but incomplete and of questionable usefulness. Indeed, there would be a missing link. Why would the absence of men stimulate this kind of interaction? Why would the women choose to discuss past hurts and disappointments by men at that very moment? The third choice provides that link and constitutes one of those rare interpretations that, together with an intellectual explanation, enables the group members to remain close to their feelings. I personally favor the first alternative, which was to say nothing. Indeed, the issues discussed were important and the women were in touch with some intense feelings and were expressing them openly and clearly. The fact that they were free to do so because of the absence of men was secondary and could be dealt with at another time.

This last example is somewhat out of place in that it does not illustrate possible alternatives. It does, however, show how perceptive the group may be on its own and seems a fitting way to end this section.

Ted, a 35-year-old graduate student, was very much in love with his wife of 10 years. Both Ted and his wife came from excessively poor backgrounds, and both, very bright, had managed to extricate themselves from the morass of their sociocultural milieu. Ted's wife had become a practical nurse but had stopped there, gone to work, while Ted pursued his graduate studies in clinical psychology. Ted had completed all other requirements but had tried in vain for almost two years to get a dissertation going. As he was expressing his discouragement, almost desperation, to us, I remember feeling very confused. I knew how much Ted loved his wife and obtaining his degree was certainly a step toward an easier life for both of them. I wanted to tell him something but did not know what. At that moment, Sherry, another graduate student, somewhat younger than Ted, stood up and went to sit next to him. She put her arm around him, smiled and said "Hey, Ted, she'll love you just as much with your Ph.D. as without it. Besides, you don't have to have children right away. She can go back to school while you work." Ted nodded gravely and the group seemed to perfectly understand and agree with Sherry's statements. I remained somewhat sheepish and marveling once again at that collective wisdon.

Feedback and Confrontation

In special groupings, such as the military, academia, and the world of therapy, many terms often acquire a surplus meaning sometimes different from the consensually agreed upon definition. It is therefore appropriate to define these two concepts as used here so that the reader understands the phenomena to which they refer.

FEEDBACK. Feedback is defined as any reaction of the group as a whole or of individual group members to another member's behavior. The feedback can be verbal or nonverbal; it may be spontaneous or come as a result of a group member's request. The group member's behavior bringing forth such feedback can also be verbal or nonverbal. It is clear that the term *feedback* is used here in a very broad sense and encompasses reactions as diverse as a show of affection, displays of anger, advice, interpretations, etc. *Confrontation* is a feedback with components of antagonism and anger and will be defined and discussed separately in the section following this one.

In the previous chapter describing the various tasks and roles of the leader, the kinds of feedback emanating from the therapist have been already discussed at length. The emphasis, in this section, will be upon appropriateness of the therapist's intervention when feedback is given by the group or individual group members.

Feedback as a Show of Affection.   The rule governing my intervention when members give feedback to each other is to stay out of the picture. This is particularly true when that feedback is supportive and affectionate. The difficulty inherent in giving and receiving affection has already been discussed. When group members reach the point when they have overcome these difficulties, the merit for such achievement should be theirs alone. Quite often, even a minimal intervention of the leader, be it praise or acknowledgement of the affection offered, may defuse the situation and prevent two people from fully experiencing the exquisite sensation of giving and receiving. There are, of course, exceptions to all rules and the one that readily comes to mind is the instance when affection is given and not received. Even then, the leader's intervention has to be finely balanced, describing what is happening and avoiding judgment or criticism.

> A training group of professional mental health workers adopted a format where members-in-training would alternate leading the group. One-third of the time, at the end, was devoted to a debriefing session. Two of the members worked together in the same agency, and there had always been some unverbalized tension between them. On that particular day, one of them was going through a fairly stressful experience. The other tried, somewhat clumsily, to express her support two or three times but her advances were ignored. In exasperation, she finally said "Is it so hard to believe that I care for you?" After a brief silence, the second member said "I just can't believe it." After a while, the leader made the following comment:
> "You both were so honest and took such a risk. It is not easy to reach for someone else. It is, perhaps, even more difficult to push away such support when that is what one honestly feels."
> That simple statement, acknowledging the behavior of both members, was sufficient to alleviate some of the tension.

Feedback as Advice.   I have found, over the years, that although advice is not as meaningful as other kinds of feedback, it serves, nevertheless, an important purpose. It gives the person who provides the advice the feeling of motion rather than immobility, a feeling that something is being done. There are few things more damaging to an individual's self-concept than inactivity, even when the activity is not very productive. It gives the person who receives the advice a feeling of being recognized and not ignored. Even if the advice is worthless, someone has paid attention. Occasionally, the advice is meaningful and helpful. On the other hand, advice giving may simply be a device to satisfy the narcissistic needs of the person who gives it or the dependency needs of the one who receives it; at other times, it may be a way of avoiding the here-and-now. At such times, it is incumbent upon the leader to point out what is happening. The group's awareness of the appropriateness and purpose of advice is an interesting phenomenon. As an example, the reader can turn to the case of Nancy described in Chapter 2 (see p. 35). To briefly summarize its salient points, Nancy was an attractive 42-year-old who had been told by two physicians that she needed to undergo a double mastectomy. With the help of the group, which was able to grasp her need to get in touch with her despair and fear, Nancy had met those feelings and had been able to cry. The group then settled in to a discussion of Nancy's condition in a practical and matter-of-fact fashion. At the advice of the group, Nancy went to an internationally known specialist and was able to avoid that tragic and disfiguring operation. In her case, the advice was pertinent, appropriate and a group endeavor.

The following illustrates a less appropriate dispensing of advice:

> In that particular group, Ginger, a young woman in her early twenties, arrived very upset and shared with the group her fear of being pregnant. Raised a Catholic, Ginger maintained many of her church's beliefs and, although considering a possible abortion, the prospect was, to her, very painful and anxiety provoking. It was quite obvious that, at the moment, all she needed was to share her fears with the group. Sy and Jean, two very religious group members, albeit of different faiths, began to bombard

> Ginger with moralistic and self-righteous advice. Ginger very
> quickly stopped talking and an embarrassed silence followed. I
> turned to Ginger and asked "Is that what you wanted to hear?"
> She shook her head while two tears rolled down her cheeks.
> Betsy, an older woman, who had remained silent until then,
> moved over to Ginger, put her head on her breast and said "It's
> all right, child, whatever happens will be all right."

Feedback as Interpretations.   Interpretations made by the group
leader have already been discussed earlier in this chapter. In the
case of interpretations made by group members to group members, I try to follow the principles outlined above. I intervene
only when interpretations are used as an avoidance of the here-
and-now. In addition, however, I remain on the alert for the
rare instances when easily influenced members are fed dangerous and/or inaccurate interpretations by another group member:

> Genevieve was an intelligent but somewhat self-centered and
> domineering young woman. She had just graduated from the
> local university with a graduate degree in counseling and felt
> compelled to act as a therapist. Maria, on the other hand, was
> fairly unsophisticated and somewhat gullible. She was sharing
> with us an argument that she had with her mother, the nature
> of which is not relevant to the discussion. Genevieve turned to
> Marie and said "That's a lot of bull. The trouble is that you're
> jealous because your mother gets to be with your old man all the
> time and you can't keep him all to yourself. At your age, you
> should be over wanting to sleep with your father." There was,
> indeed, some truth in Genevieve's statement. The interpretation,
> however, was made brutally and inappropriately. Maria began
> to cry and said "I don't think so, but if you say so, why . . . that
> is horrible." I turned to Genevieve and stated (somewhat more
> harshly than I had intended) "For God's sake, Genevieve, stop
> playing psychiatrist." The motivations for my statement were, of
> course, multiple and not altogether due to my concern for Ma-
> ria's welfare. . . . The fact remained that Maria seemed greatly
> relieved and much less anxious.

Feedback as Information About One's Self.   This is, perhaps, the
most important, yet the most abused and potentially harmful

kind of feedback. It is a truism to say that they way we are perceived and experienced by other people determines to a great extent their behavior toward us. Unless we are aware of how we affect others, it is difficult to correctly interpret their reactions to us. Misinterpreting their responses affects our behavior, creating the vicious cycle and the distortion that continues to grow. The following brief example illustrates this point.

> Marjorie was a very shy, frightened young woman, convinced that she was so insignificant that people would not think it worthwhile to pay attention to her or want to spend any time interacting with her. She would, therefore, avoid the company of others, walk looking straight ahead with a very serious mien, and refuse to participate in social activities. Marjorie was a very beautiful, tall, regal person and those who worked with and interacted with her felt that she was haughty, conceited, and aloof. They avoided her, thus reinforcing Majrorie's perception of herself as an insignificant person and she isolated herself even more.

In order to establish some accurate perspective to the above situation, Marjorie should have known that she was seen as aloof and haughty rather than scared and shy, and she was perceived and experienced that way because of specific behaviors in which she engaged, i.e., avoiding people, not greeting them, not participating in social activities, etc.

The group is, perhaps, the only forum where several people at once are concerned enough to provide that kind of feedback, thus enabling the person to correctly assess the impact one has on others and, if desired, to take the necessary steps to correct that impact. It is also potentially harmful for the following reasons. The feedback may be inaccurate and no more than a projection of the individual who gives the feedback. This is particularly dangerous when that group member is charismatic and has leadership abilities. In such cases, the person to whom the feedback is addressed or even the group may have a difficult time challenging the feedback. The group member may accept the inaccurate information about him- or herself, act upon it, and increase the dissonance that one experiences when the discrepancy increases the between what one is and what one tries to be.

Another harmful potential of feedback about the self has to do with the manner in which that feedback is delivered. It must be remembered that, quite often, the manner in which people behave serves and has served a protective purpose. Even when the original danger is no longer present, to remove that protection too harshly or too suddenly might be frightening and may strip the person of his or her dignity and self-respect. The possibility was discussed by Koch (1972) in a rather exaggerated yet thought-provoking criticism of encounter groups. His words are worth quoting as he refers to an academic man who, in an encounter group, had been given some painful feedback.

> Is it not possible that this "perceptive" and contained man was pressured into relinquishing something gallant and proud in his make up? Is it not conceivable that even if disclosure had made him feel somewhat better, he had become somewhat less? (p. 41)

In order to be accepted and integrated by the person, feedback about the self (provided, of course, that feedback is accurate) should be given in a gentle, supportive, and respectful manner. If given in a harsh, humiliating, and demeaning way, the person will probably reject it in anger. If accepted, he or she will feel belittled, hurt, even, at times, devastated. I make the point very clear to the members of my group and, at the risk of sounding corny, I make the following analogy.

> Sometimes, an otherwise attractive and well-dressed woman may be unaware that her slip is showing. Most people will not care enough to tell her and she will go on with that flaw. Some people may mock and ridicule her and, if this happens, the woman may not believe them or she will believe them and feel angry and humiliated. Some people may care enough to tell her in a gentle and respectful manner. At such times, the woman will

probably believe them, be thankful, and repair the flaw in her attire. I hope that in our group we shall care enough about each other to honestly tell each other when our slips are showing. I hope that we shall do so in a manner that will enable us to appreciate the feedback and make us want to do something about it.

In addition to such straightforward information, the group leader may engage in additional interventions to insure that feedback about the self be productive and not harmful.

The group leader must ascertain that the feedback represents a consensus and not simply a projection of individual group members. This is illustrated in the following:

Renee was an unusually intelligent and perceptive woman in her forties who, as a child, had experienced severe rejection by both parents, especially her father. At the age of 18, motivated by the desire to leave a very traumatic environment, she married a man as rejecting as her father and who delighted in repeatedly humiliating and berating her. While profoundly unhappy, she always thought that a male, in order to be a "real man" had to be brutal and inconsiderate. Eventually, after several months of individual therapy, she decided to divorce her husband and, later, married a gentle, kind, and supportive individual. Several years later, she decided to join a group. She had a happy conjugal life but had not been able to totally overcome her suspicions of and antagonisms toward men. Alfred, another member of the group, of approximately the same age as Renee, was an unusually shy and reserved individual with a rather low self-concept, always concerned about not offending anyone, especially woman, who terrified him. On that particular day, he was sharing with us his disappointment and hurt at having lost an excellent secretary who had resigned without warning and/or explanation. Renee turned to him and said "You men are all alike. You probably treated her like a piece of furniture. No wonder she up and left." Alfred become very agitated. At that moment, another female group member stated "That is not true. I don't believe it. You are a hell of a nice guy and we all love you." That comment was echoed by the other group members and Renee, remembering her early experiences with men, was quick to acknowledge that

> she really did not mean what she had said and admitted that she had a tendency to become hostile whenever she felt that another woman was being attacked. (*N.B.* If supportive statements had not been forthcoming, I would have asked Renee to check with the rest of the group and determine whether they agreed with her.)

If the feedback is accurate, the group leader should never undo it by disagreeing with it. If, however, the feedback is given in a hostile, destructive manner, the group leader should balance it by offering the recipient of the feedback an ego-syntonic, supportive comment about him or her provided, of course, that comment be accurate:

> Joseph was a Lutheran minister. A handsome, sensitive man in his early forties, he had a tendency to pontificate in an irritating manner. During that one session, he had been particularly verbose and Dorothy, an outgoing and very direct woman, stated "I wish the hell you would stop sounding like a preacher all the time. This really pisses me off. Can't you just talk like a regular person?" Joseph was taken aback, and, when Dorothy's statements were echoed by the group, his face reddened, he looked very upset, and there were tears in his eyes. That aspect of Joseph, that is, his sensitivity to feedback was new to us. There was an embarrassed silence and I stated "You have a gift with words, Joseph, and you always mean what you say. It is only a matter of saying it in a different way." Joseph gave me a grateful look and, addressing himself to Dorothy, replied "I know I get carried away sometimes, but I'll really try."

The therapist must always remember that the goal in giving a person feedback about him- or herself is not to coerce that person to change or conform to a certain set of norms. It is only to render the person aware of how he or she is perceived and experienced by others and of the specific behaviors that led to that perception and experience. True, the above statement may be considered somewhat hypocritical in that the individual receiving negative feedback has to change certain behaviors in order to elicit a more positive response. I try, however, to limit my feedback to simple information, to avoid putting pressure for change on anyone, and I try to accept the fact that people change their behaviors at different rates and some choose not to change at all.

CONFRONTATION.   Confrontation is defined as an angry reaction of one group member to another. Sometimes, the demarcation line between a confrontation and negative feedback about the self is difficult to establish. There may, indeed, be a considerable amount of anger in negative feedback. Perhaps, the one differentiating factor is the personalized aspect of the confrontation. Except in the very rare cases when the group as a whole is angry at one member, confrontation as the term is used here, is a one-to-one interaction that does not necessarily require group consensus.

> Toni and Beth were both educated and intelligent women but at opposite poles in terms of social and political beliefs. During that particular session, the topic was on premarital sex, and Toni related with a great deal of feeling the experience of a very close friend who, after having had premarital intercourse, was going through some severe guilt and anxiety. Beth made the statement that had Toni's friend abstained from premarital intercourse, she would have saved herself a great deal of pain. Toni became very angry. Until that time, the two women had tolerated each other and had had little direct contact. Toni exploded "I've just about had enough. I'm sick of your pious, self-righteous attitudes . . ." and went on for a while in the same vein. Beth replied in kind, and the exchange was angry, open, and quite personal. After the anger was expressed, with the group's help, Toni and Beth talked about themselves and their experiences. They both realized that each experienced a great deal of ambivalence in their respective views, and, in some interesting ways, each was envious of the other. The confrontation became the beginning of a good friendship.

As little boys become good friends only after a knockdown, drag-out fight, group members who confront each other honestly learn to respect and get close to each other. The confrontation clears the air, reestablishes an open communication often inhibited by unverbalized feelings of anger and resentment.

What is the role of the leader in the event of confrontation between group members? As a rule, I follow the principle governing interventions that I outlined at the beginning of the section on *feedback,* i.e., I stay out of the picture. I try to provide an example and to suggest some informal rules for healthy confrontation. I confront the other person with the effects of his or her behavior on me but do not impugn that person's motivation. For example, I may say "You are not hearing what I am saying and this pisses me off." But, I will not say "You don't care enough to hear what I am saying." I will not be ambiguous in confronting the other person with my feelings and will do so either by informing the person or by "being" my feeling. For example, I will say "Your not listening to me makes me furious" or "Dammit, listen to me." The only instances when I intervene actively in cases of confrontation are when a group member attempts to enlist the help of and incite the rest of the group against a particular group member. These instances are rare. The group, in its collective wisdom, refuses to allow itself to be used in that manner. They may occur, however, especially when the inciting member has a strong and charismatic personality. At such times, I may intervene in order to avoid scapegoating, one of the most painful, humiliating, and devastating experiences in a group. Such an example is described here:

> Tall, bearded, with a winning smile and a booming voice, Jimmy was highly verbal and alternated between charming and intimidating the rest of the group. The only group member who consistently challenged him was Henrietta, a rather nondescript, but spunky young woman. As Jimmy was pontificating on an unimportant topic, Henrietta interrupted him, and Jimmy became quite angry at her and, addressing himself to the rest of the group, stated "Don't you think I'm right? She is always inconsid-

erate and only concerned with her own feelings. She won't believe me, so you tell her ..." The group squirmed somewhat
uncomfortably and sided with Jimmy, attacking Henrietta in a
half-hearted way. Yet, the comments were unfair, and it was
obvious that Henrietta had a difficult time holding her own. I
interrupted the action and said "Jimmy, I won't go into whether
you are right or wrong regarding Henrietta. This is between the
two of you. I wonder what made you enlist everybody's help?"
My comments were sufficient to prevent further scapegoating.

Transference and Counter-Transference

Within the context of this book, the concepts of transference and counter-transference are ascribed a somewhat
broader, albeit not much different, meaning from that generally
accepted and described by Anna Freud (1954). Each concept
will, therefore, be defined so that the phenomena to which they
refer may be clearly understood.

TRANSFERENCE.   Transference is defined as a group member's
reaction to another group member, or to the group leader, for
which there is no group consensus. This reaction can be positive
or negative. Often, such reactions are so idiosyncratic that the
group member is hesitant to express them, especially when he
or she believes that the reactions will be unpopular, such as
negative feelings toward a well-liked member or strong sexual
feelings toward a group member of the opposite sex. Whether
or not transferential feelings will be expressed in the group
depends greatly upon the prevailing milieu. The safer the group
atmosphere, the greater the likelihood that such feelings will be
expressed without special encouragement or prompting from
the leader. Occasionally, a group member may feel rebuffed and
rejected at the realization that his or her perception of another
group member is not shared by the rest of the group. At such
times, I become more active and encourage the group member
to express all feelings regardless of what they may be and to
check for group consensus. I explain that such feelings are not

bizarre but are activated because, in some unknown way, the person who expresses them is reminded by the other group member of an important person in his or her life who had originally generated such feelings. The concept of transference is very quickly understood and accepted by group members. Eventually, instead of berating a group member for seemingly irrational feelings, the group will work very hard at searching for the origin of the transferential feelings. I feel it is important that group members learn, as much as possible, to differentiate between transferential and nontransferential feelings. I feel it is less important to attempt to work through the transference in the group. By "working through," I mean attempting to resolve the relationship between the group member and the important person in that member's life who was the original and legitimate recipient of the feelings expressed in the group. I usually attempt such resolution through the use of psychodramatic techniques, and I am always careful to ask the consent not only of the person involved but also of the rest of the group because a considerable amount of time may be devoted to only one person. The following examples illustrate the concepts described above:*

> Donna and Bernie were as dissimilar as two women can be. Donna, in her late forties, was pleasant to look at, serious, with a lot of depth. Bernie, in her late twenties, was unusually pretty, flirtatious, and somewhat superficial. Donna had owned up to some very complex feelings toward Bernie, often angry and resentful, yet at other times overprotective. She was aware of the fact that Bernie reminded her of her younger sister who had died several years before in a plane crash. One evening, at my suggestion and with the concurrence of the group, Donna attempted to explore in greater depth her feelings toward her dead sister. The drama that unfolded was a moving experinece. Bernie, of course, played the part of Donna's sister and two other members

*Another interaction between Donna and Bernie was described earlier in this book in a different context. Chronologically the drama described here occurred much later than the exchange mentioned in Chapter 1.

became Donna's parents. Donna was able to become very angry at her parents for having always compared the two sisters to Donna's disadvantage. She verbalized her jealousy at her sister for "taking all the boys," and for being so attractive. She owned up to her death wishes toward her sister and her terrible guilt at her sister's death. At the end of the drama, Donna told her sister how much she loved her and how good she felt at having been able to tell her all this and still know that they could love each other. By that time, the whole group (including, I believe, the director) were in tears. From that day on, the relationship between Donna and Bernie changed gradually. Donna became more honestly angry at Bernie, and Bernie began to look up to Donna and to model herself after her, becoming less flirtatious, and less superficial. When Bernie left the group, she and Donna had become quite close to each other.

I had suffered a fairly severe case of food poisoning, but, since it was too late to cancel the group, I tried to make the session anyway. Within ten minutes into the session, I had a violent stomach spasm and, unable to say a word, rushed to the bathroom. Alex, a young physician, followed me to the bathroom and persuaded me to let him drive me home. Since, by that time, I was violently ill, it did not take much persuasion. When Alex returned to the group to inform them of what happened, he found them all anxious, of course, but Edith, a young Israeli student, was beside herself with worry and very angry at me and berated me for being so inconsiderate and insensitive to everybody's feelings. When the group pointed out the absurdity of her complaint, Edith insisted that her feelings, although unreasonable, were strong and real. With the group's help, Edith talked about the sudden death of her father, as a result of a heart attack, when Edith was a little girl. She smiled and said, addressing herself to me, "I guess I do feel like your little girl, sometimes, but I'll get over it."

In the first example described above, Donna was aware of the transferential aspects of her feelings and used the group to work through them by bringing some resolution to the relationship with her dead sister. In the second example, Edith became aware of the nature of her feelings toward me but chose not to deal with the death of her father.

COUNTER-TRANSFERENCE.   Counter-transference is defined as feelings experienced by the group leader toward members of the group for which there seems to be no apparent reason. The group leader must be particularly attentive to such feelings, especially of a negative nature and of how they affect his or her behavior. Indeed, erratic behavior on the part of the leader, especially when not acknowledged, may breed insecurity among group members and affect the leader's credibility. When such feelings occur, it is entirely possible that they may be transient and caused by the mood of the moment. If they do not dissipate, then it is incumbent upon the leader to discuss them with a colleague and try to get at the bottom of them. In the very rare instances, when this is not possible, then the group leader must share his or her feelings with the group, being particularly careful to assume responsibility for them and to not project them onto the group members.

I remember, with some amusement and fondness, being bothered by some protective feelings that I was experiencing for a young social worker who had joined our group. I was discussing them with a colleague in my office, and, on my desk, I had a picture of my wife when I had first met her 26 years earlier. My colleague who knew the social worker (in fact, he had referred her to me) said nothing and simply pointed at the picture. For the first time, I became aware of the strong resemblance. I shared that experience with the group who seemed quite appreciative and, laughingly, one group member stated "It's OK, we won't let you protect her too much. She'll take her bumps same as the rest of us."

Socializing Outside the Group

Socialization outside the group is a matter of controversy. Some group leaders encourage it while others go to the other extreme and expressly forbid it. The rationale for that extreme position is that, by talking to someone outside of the group, issues that should be brought to the group will be defused. It is hardly plausible that a person will run out of conflictual issues simply because of the opportunity to talk about them outside of the group. Indeed, people in analysis find enough to talk about five hours a week over several years. Besides, the person who wants to talk to someone will always manage to find a receptive ear. It is equally absurd to forbid liaisons between group members. In the first place, if two group members wish to have an intimate relationship, and this is not approved by the group leader, they will simply engage into it without telling the group. In addition, I do not believe that a group leader has the right to rule, in any way, the activities of group members outside of the group room.

Socialization outside the group can, at times, afford a network of peer support not unlike Alcoholics Anonymous (AA). Twice in my 15 years of practice, deeply depressed and suicidal group members, unwilling to contact another therapist whose name I had given them, were prevented from harming themselves by the support provided by the rest of the group whom they were able to contact while I was out of the country on vacation. While I do not actively support this kind of intermember network, I do not discourage it, either.

My own socialization with group members is limited to occasional group activities such as a Christmas party or a party to celebrate a group member's termination. I believe that a group leader should curtail social activities outside of the group situation. Such self-imposed limitations, however, may be lifted after members terminate therapy. The fact that a person has, at one time, been a therapist's patient does not mean that, henceforth, therapist and client belong to two separate worlds. After the therapist–client relationship has ended, therapist and client may relate as people, and several of my group members have remained good friends for many years after they have left the group.

Such are the issues with which I have often struggled. There are, I am sure, many more that can come up in the life of the group and not all can be predicted and discussed. As

stated at the beginning of this section, the therapist who encounters new situations will have to use his or her judgment and
intuition tempered by his concern for the group members.

SUMMARY

Behavior and responsibilities of the leader, not discussed
in the preceding chapter, were divided into two categories:
Logistics and *Clinical Issues.*

I. Logistics

The Logistics of leading a group include

1. *Interviewing and choosing group members*
2. *The contract*

The Contract should clearly specify the obligations of the
leader as well as of the group members.

    A. *The group leader's obligations.* They include:
        a) A description of the process
        b) The therapist's presence and an adequate
           meeting room
        c) The therapist's total involvement
        d) Availability and confidentiality
    B. *The member's obligations.* They are related to:
        a) Confidentiality
        b) Attendance
        c) Freedom
        d) Socializing outside the group
        e) Payment of fees

II. Clinical Issues

Clinical issues discussed include:

1. *Interpretations versus acknowledging the group process.*
2. *Feedback and confrontation*
    A. *Feedback:* There are different kinds of feedback
        as follows:
        a) Feedback as a show of affection
        b) Feedback as advice

       c)   Feedback as interpretation

       d)   Feedback as information about the self

   B.   *Confrontation:* It is defined as an idiosyncratic feedback with components of anger.

3.   *Transference and counter-transference*

   A.   *Transference:* It is defined as a group member's reaction to another group member or to the leader for which there is no group consensus.

   B.   *Counter-transference:* It is defined as feelings experienced by the group leader toward members of the group for which there seems to be no apparent reason.

4.   *Socializing outside the group*

Chapter 6

ODDS AND ENDS

We are now nearing the end of the road. I tried and hopefully succeeded to be cohesive and describe one approach to group therapy in an organized and understandable fashion. I began with building a case for group therapy, developed a theory to account for what happens in groups, and described the nature of the group process. I, then, was specific in describing the role of the leader and ended with the logistics of group therapy practice and the discussion of several clinical issues. There are a few topics that must still be discussed, such as the qualifications necessary for being a group therapist, some clinical issues that I found important enough to be discussed separately, and, finally a brief section on how to start and maintain a private practice in group therapy. The last topic overlaps and should be read together with the section on logistics. I chose to insert it in this chapter, separately from the section on logistics, because it is less general and refers specifically to private practice.

WHO WILL LEAD

It is obvious by now that to be a competent group leader is no easy task. The raw material with which a group leader works, for example, the thoughts, feelings, overt behavior, and ultimately, the peace of mind of other human beings, is a far too precious commodity to be tampered with lightly. It is, therefore, somewhat ironic and frightening to realize that there is no consensus regarding the qualifications of a group therapist while, on the other hand, society requires some stringent criteria of competence for an engineer, a chemist, or even a public relations person. In the 1960s self-appointed group leaders of all sorts of growth, encounter, human potential groups, etc. proliferated. The divergence of views regarding requirements for a group therapist is reflected on one hand in Schutz's statement as quoted by Jane Howard to the effect that vibrations are very important to disqualify potential leaders (Howard, 1970) and on the other by Lakin's (1970) contrasting opinion that people who train trainers should hold advanced degrees, such as the Ph.D., the M.D., or the Ed.D., while trainers themselves should hold the equivalent of a Master's degree and, in addition, meet a number of assorted criteria. It is only within the past 10 years that the two major organizations of group therapy, The American Group Psychotherapy Association (AGPA) and the American Society for Group Psychotherapy and Psychodrama (ASGPP) have begun to deal seriously with the problem and establish guidelines for training and requirements for certification. Those guidelines and requirements will be briefly described later.

The primary purpose of this chapter, however, is to discuss some of the characteristics of a group therapist and to suggest a model for training. Three areas of the leader's functioning will be discussed and all three are believed to be equally important. These are the leader's personality, training, and ethics. Because it is impossible to describe the tasks of the leader without discussing the leader, much of the content of this chapter has been alluded to earlier in a somewhat scattered fashion. I believe it useful and necessary, however, to pull together these characteristics of the leader not only within the context of the various aspects of the leader's performance but within the context of what a leader is expected to know and expected to be.

THE LEADER'S PERSONALITY

It has become apparent from the discussion of the leader's tasks that much of the leader's performance can be described concretely and can be learned through study and repetition. A great part of the leader's success depends upon the self of that leader and the way in which that self is used. Hence the distinction between what a leader does and what a leader is, and between training and personality. The distinction, of course, is not always clearcut. Indeed, as will be suggested later, a group leader may learn to modify and use in a better way some aspects of his or her personality. Such learning, however, when it occurs, is acquired in a less concrete fashion than the more mechanical aspects of the leader's performance.

The Accepting Leader

The pivotal assumption upon which this theory of group therapy rests is that an accepting and supportive milieu liberates the individual from the fear of recognizing and communicating openly his or her thoughts and feelings. The various ways in which such an environment may be promoted have been discussed at length in Chapter 4. Yet, even a compulsive adherence to the guidelines and principles outlined in that chapter will be insufficient if the group leader is basically rejecting and intolerant of other people. Perhaps this statement bears more discussion as it may be easily misunderstood. I am not speaking of the unrealistic, universal love preached by major religions. Admirable as that concept may be, it is not pragmatic and often becomes a source of guilt for many people who believe that they should (and yet cannot) love one and all. I am speaking of the belief, both at an intellectual and emotional level, that people are important and entitled to a basic care and liking; that among their inalienable rights are the right to be treated with dignity and respect by all other people. I am speaking also, of the ability to resonate to another person's sadness, grief, and even joy. In short, I am speaking of a therapeutic personality as eloquently described by Rogers (1961). I firmly believe that a person prone to look down upon others, who experiences no pleasure in the company of others, who remains unaffected by other people's emotions should find other fields of endeavor, and abstain from becoming a group therapist.

Can these characteristics be taught? Attempts have, of course, been made in that direction but the data are inconclusive (Naar, 1970; Truax & Carkhuff, 1967). It appears that, through careful training, potential leaders can learn to become less possessive, more tolerant of other people, and more in touch with their feelings. I doubt, however, that a basic liking for and a responsiveness to people can be taught through an academic process. It is my belief that they can only be learned through life experiences or through psychotherapy.

Awareness of One's Needs and the Ability to Differentiate Them from the Needs of the Clients

It was stated in a preceding chapter that a leader must be a model but should also avoid preempting his or her clients and should avoid using the group directly to solve his or her personal problems. It becomes, therefore, necessary that the leader be aware of his or her feelings and needs, not only when socially acceptable, but also when such needs and feelings clash with the therapist's self-concept. This is a painful but necessary process. Awareness of one's feelings and needs enables the therapist to curb them (or seek help elsewhere for them) rather than satisfy them at the expense of the group or to adversely affect the group by an unhealthy defense against an unrecognized need as illustrated below:

Dr. J. was a psychiatric resident whom I had had the pleasure of supervising. She was an unusually sensitive, intuitive, and gentle woman, very much liked by her patients. One day, she arrived quite upset to our supervisory session and explained that when an argument broke out in her group, she had become quite upset and stopped it abruptly. She was very justly concerned that her failure to allow the argument to develop would damage her credibility with the members of the group and establish undesirable and not very healthy norms. During our conversation, Dr. J. talked about her fears of confrontation and related them to some of her early experiences. Her fear of confrontation was not, of course, a new awareness. What was new was the realization of the extent to which she was ruled by it in the group. She became sensitized to her reaction and, when another confrontation arose, she allowed it to develop. This was difficult for her but became easier as time went on. Toward the end of our supervisory relationship, she stated "Confrontation is still difficult for me, and probably always will remain so. But now, I am aware of the discomfort and I can control it."

Charles, a graduate student, had spent sometime with a Gestalt group on the West Coast. He had mastered the jargon and some of the techniques of Gestalt therapy but lacked both in sensitivity and knowledge of personality and human behavior. While leading the group, he was pompous and tended to use grandiloquent and, sometimes, obscure expressions; he basked in the admiration of group members who were awed by a language that they could not understand. Eventually, a new member joined the group. More assertive than the others, he challenged Charles and asked him "to quit the bullshit and talk so that we can understand you." Charles became very upset, especially when the group sided with the new member. He felt let down, betrayed, refused to face the possibility that the new member may have been right. He lost credibility with the group. The group lost its awe of Charles. He left the group, at termination of his internship, and stated that he had gone through one of the most miserable experiences of his student days.

In the first example, Dr. J. was aware of her fear of confrontation. She could have chosen to eliminate or discourage confrontation at the expense of the group's open communication. Instead, she chose to talk about her fear with a fellow professional, was able to curb it, and did not inhibit the communication in her group. Charles, on the other hand, could not own up to his insecurity, his need for being looked up to. The results were a traumatic experience for him and probably for the members of the group as well.

The ways in which a group leader fails to differentiate his or her needs from those of the group are many and quite subtle. A group leader may erroneously assume that his or her feelings or needs are shared by the group and act accordingly. A group leader may be so wrapped up in him- or herself that not only will he or she not be sensitive to the needs of the group but may preempt the members and use the group to fulfill his or her own needs. I believe that all group therapists, especially at the beginning of their careers, have at one time or another made such mistakes. I remember being tired and cutting a session short, having convinced myself that the group members were tired also. I remember arriving at a group session in a joyous mood and being unable to resonate to (in fact, being somewhat indignant at) the sad mood of the group. Preempting group members, another way of not differentiating one's feelings from the feelings of the group, was discussed at length in Chapter 4.

It is illusory to believe that one can be, at all times, attuned to one's own needs and always able to differentiate them from the needs of others. On the other hand, there are some persons so narcissisitcally involved in themselves and so impervious to the needs and feelings of other people that they go through life like a bull through a china shop. They should stay away from the field of group therapy. Most, however, present and potential group therapists can learn through time, experience, and through the wisdom of fellow therapists and group members. It is important, however, to recognize that we have things to learn. Some of us must learn to feel comfortable with confronting and with being confronted; some of us must learn to give and to receive affection and some of us must cope with the fear and the pain of rejection. And if all the learning cannot take place, the recognition that it is needed will prevent us from damaging the people who have placed their trust in us.

Awareness of One's Impact upon Group Members

The tremendous importance that a group leader acquires for the members of the group has already been discussed in Chapter 4. Partly because of operating transferences, partly because of legitimate expectations, the leader is endowed with characteristics and qualities that are, sometimes, sheer fantasy and almost always exaggerated. Transferences and expectations are not the only two factors that determine how the leader is perceived. The leader's objective characteristics are also important as they interact with transferences and expectation. It is, therefore, important that a group leader be aware of such charactersitics. To use a somewhat inelegant but eloquent expression, the group leader must know how he or she "comes across." Such knowledge will be helpful in understanding group members' reactions and the extent to which such reactions are realistic or not.

The "Prejudiced" Leader

The struggle of black Americans for civil rights and the valiant fight of women for equality have sensitized many of us, not only to specific problems and hurts experienced by minorities, but also to the many subtle ways in which our conscious and unconscious attitudes continue to perpetuate this state of affairs. Many believe that if the therapist belongs to the same category of people as the group members, he or she will resonate better to their problems, and the harmful effects of the attitudes described above will be avoided. There has been a trend in the past several years to encourage a woman therapist for women, a black therapist for black group members, etc. Except in such cases where the group meets for a specific purpose such as to examine issues of sex role definition within the context of the same sex group (Bernardez & Stein, 1979) I do not believe that this approach is truly fruitful. If that concept is pushed to its logical extreme, then there would be a women's group led by a woman, an addicts' group led by an addict, a group for blacks led by a black, Jewish or Catholic groups led by a Jewish or Catholic therapist, and so on. Even if that were possible, such a fragmentation would further augment the disunity of a society already divided against itself. On the other hand, the issue of therapist's prejudice is real and potentially harmful. It is rare that one can be free of prejudices. It is possible, however, to be aware of one's prejudices and face them honestly. If such prejudices can be overcome, then this will lead to therapist's maturity and growth. If it cannot be overcome, then it is incumbent on the part of the ethical therapist not to work with people against whom he or she harbors an unsurmountable prejudice. If a person feels more comfortable working with a therapist of the same sex, race, or religion or if a therapist feels more at ease with clients of the same sex, race, or religion, they should, of course, be encouraged to follow their preferences. My earnest hope is that the day will come when all people will be comfortable with each other. Pain and joy, sadness and happiness, anger and love are universal and know no boundaries of sex, race, national origin, or religious affiliation.

THE LEADER'S TRAINING

Out of the painful confusion of the 1960s, some consensus and formal guidelines began to emerge. The two major umbrella organizations, the American Group Psychotherapy Association (AGPA) and the American Society for Group Psychotherapy and Psychodrama (ASGPP) took a commendable lead and the first printing of the AGPA's *Guidelines for the*

Training of Group Psychotherapists appeared in 1970 and the latest revision appeared in 1978. Essentially, the AGPA guidelines suggest a generic training in a mental health profession to be followed by a rigorous program of training of a two-year minimum duration. An interesting aspect of the suggested training program is the trainee's participation in group psychotherapy for a minimum of 120 hours. The suggested training program is geared to meet the requirements for associate membership in the American Group Psychotherapy Association. Additional requirements of direct treatment and supervision will lead to full membership in the organization.

The ASGPP chose to follow a somewhat different approach. Shortly after the death of Moreno, the society empowered a board of senior Directors to survey credentials, conduct appropriate examinations, and confer to applicants a certificate as a practitioner or as a trainer, educator, and practitioner in Psychodrama, Sociometry and Group Psychotherapy according to the applicant's level of expertise. After the initial tenure, members of the board have been elected by the society's membership, and the board is known as the American Board of Examiners in Psychodrama, Sociometry, and Group Psychotherapy. Requirements for admission to candidacy include a generic training in a mental health profession also followed by a very exacting program of training in psychodrama. The program may span more than two years, but the applicant must be able to account for a given number of hours of training. Admission to candidacy is followed by the appropriate examination. In addition to certification of individuals, the Board of Examiners also certifies training institutions by reviewing the credentials of the teaching staff and the quality of training offered. The AGPA guidelines for training as well as the ASGPP requirements for certification are well thought out and meet a crying need for the protection of the consumer. It is regrettable that neither the AGPA guidelines nor the ASGPP requirements emphasize the therapist's personality as an important criterion. The AGP's guidelines, suggesting that the trainee attend a goup as a patient, come closest to implying that the therapist's personality is important, although the reason given for that guideline is only that "a therapist should have an experience comparable to a patient's experience in an ongoing group" (AGPA, 1978).

In a recent article (Naar, 1979), I outlined a model for the training of therapists and the practice of psychotherapy. This model, based on three assumptions, can with some slight modifications, be used for the training of group therapists and the practice of group psychotherapy and is described below:

Assumptions

1. A supportive environment, as described in Chapters 2 and 4 facilitates open communication and enhances a desirable process. An open communication brings about changes in self-concept and in the nature of one's interpersonal relationships.
2. Specific interventions on the part of the leader* within such a supportive milieu and a defined theoretical framework, can enhance such changes and result in additional resolutions of conflict and changes in behavior left unaffected by the supportive milieu alone.
3. Specific leader's interventions will not be effective unless used within the context of a supportive milieu.

These assumptions have implications for the teaching and practice of group therapy and, as a corollary, I am suggesting the following trilevel model both for training and practice.

Level 1.   Thorough training in human behavior, personality theory and assessment, developmental and

*Such specific interventions are the ways of enhancing a desirable process as described in Chapter 4, the use of psychodrama, Gestalt techniques, or any other approach to therapy with which a group leader is familiar.

abnormal psychology, experimental design, group dynamics and other related academic courses.

Level 2.   The extent to which candidates have a therapeutic personality (as discussed at the beginning of the chapter) will be used as an important criterion for admission to further training. Training of the candidate in enhancing a supportive milieu (the generic basis for the kind of group psychotherapy advocated here) should then take place before the candidates learn the various approaches to group.

Level 3.   Training in the various approaches to group therapy. This third level of training would begin within the context of a formal education and continue throughout the therapist's life.

It will be noticed that training at level 1 operationally describes the generic training in a mental health field required by both the AGPA and the ASGPP. It is expected that graduate training leading to the acceptable professional degree in any mental health field will cover all the above as well as many additional academic subjects. Level 3, of course, can be achieved by the training program suggested and/or required by the two organizations. It is level 2 that differentiates the above model from those advocated by AGPA and ASGPP. Indeed, not only does it require specific training in enhancing a supportive milieu, but it also suggests that the candidate's therapeutic personality be a criterion for admission to training in group therapy. The idea, of course, is not new and it is admittedly difficult to implement (Truax & Carkhuff 1967).

Training at level 1 only can produce competent students of human behavior, who are excellent researchers but not therapists. Training at level 2 or levels 2 and 3 (i.e., having neglected level 1) will produce mere technicians, often helpful, rarely damaging, but hardly achieving theirs and their client's potential.

Training at level 3 only or even levels 3 and 1, could easily produce therapists who are ineffective, and sometimes even damaging to their clients.

Parallel levels in the practice of therapy could be conceptualized as follows:

Level 1.   *Research, assessment of the client's situation, problems, and tentative goals.* Training at level 1 would qualify a mental health professional to practice at level 1.

Level 2.   *Leading nontherapy and therapy groups under supervision.* Training at level 2 or levels 2 and 1 would qualify for practice at level 2.

Level 3.   *Leading therapy groups.* Training at levels 1, 2, and 3 would qualify for the independent practice of group therapy. Group therapists, having achieved all the levels of training and flexible and knowledgeable enough to practice at all three levels, will probably be the most effective.

THE LEADER'S ETHICS

Group therapists tread on somewhat safer grounds in the area of ethics. Each of the major mental health disciplines, psychology, social work, and psychiatry, has its own satisfactory code of ethics. Since I belong to the discipline of psychology, I am guided by the *Ethical Standards of Psychologists* (American Psychological Association, 1979). There are practicing group psychotherapists who have a satisfactory generic training without belonging to any of the three major mental health disciplines and therefore, may experience the need for some ethical guidelines especially as they pertain to the practice of group therapy. Such guidelines are offered below not as a substitute but as an addition to already existing codes of ethics.

1. *The therapist will never knowingly do anything to harm group members.* It is an illusion to believe that we can always

be of help and, sometimes, in our unwillingness to face that possibility, we may resort to interventions and techniques that have not been proven and that can be potentially hazardous. A therapist may be forgiven for not being helpful, but there is no excuse for a therapist who takes chances at the expense of group members.

2. *The therapist will never use group members for self-gratification.* This guideline needs to be somewhat clarified. By virtue of leading the group, a group therapist derives many gratifications, not the least of which is to see people he or she cares about become happier. It is gratifying to be liked, to be looked up to, to be thought well of. These rewards are part of being a good group therapist and are quite legitimate. The kind of self-gratifications that would violate a therapist's professional ethics would be to use group members to satisfy one's sexual needs, for example, or to use the group directly to solve one's problems, although I consider the latter a much less severe violation than the first.

3. *The therapist will maintain him- or herself in good physical, psychological, and emotional condition.* A group therapist owes to group members his or her full attention and best efforts. This is not possible when the therapist is run down, physically ill, or under psychological and emotional stress. It is the therapist's responsibility to maintain him- or herself in such a condition that he or she can fully live up to the terms of the contract.

4. *The therapist will establish a contract clearly, make certain that the group members fully understand and accept its terms, and he or she will make every effort to live up to the terms of that contract.* The term *contract* is used here in a broad sense and includes all items discussed in Chapter 5 under the rubrique of *logistics,* for example, confidentiality, a comfortable meeting place, fees setting, etc.

I must repeat that the above sketchy guidelines should be viewed as an addition to but not as a substitution for a standard code of ethics governing the activities of a mental health professional. While they deal with some major ethical principles, they leave many areas untouched, such as the therapist's public behavior, professional relationships, research activities, etc. These areas are very important; they are, however, discussed at length in the *Ethical Standards of Psychologist,* for example, and further discussion would be redundant.

How to Start and Maintain a Successful Practice of Group Therapy

During the past several years, an increasing number of clinical psychologists have branched into private practice. The reasons for this phenomenon are many. In part, it is due to budgetary restrictions limiting opportunities in teaching and research, the two traditional activities of psychologists. Legislation permitting third-party payment to psychologists was also a contributing factor. To a large extent the increasing high quality of training and service offered by psychologists established their credibility and facilitated their increased participation in the private sector. The zeitgeist suggests that the trend will increase, and that the psychologists' example will be followed by other well trained mental health professionals such as, for instance, clinical social workers. On the other hand, the high fees asked for individual therapy place it out of reach of the average citizen even with the assistance of third party payment. As recently pointed out by Zimet (1979), individual therapy, for the same reason, is hardly expected to survive in any national health insurance plan. As individual therapy becomes less accessible and as therapists become increasingly aware of the efficacy of group therapy, it is my belief that group therapy will be the trend of the future.

Because of the increasing number of mental health practitioners in private practice and the bright future of group therapy, the following hints are offered on how to start and maintain a successful practice of group therapy. If I were to encapsulate the three main requirements for a successful practice of group therapy, I would call them *competence, ethics,* and *preparedness.* The following paragraphs will, therefore, overlap to some extent with sections of preceding chapters where these concepts have already been discussed at length. They will be looked at, however, from a somewhat different angle.

1. *The therapist must be thoroughly trained and competent in at least one approach to group therapy.* There is an unfortunate tendency among holders of an advanced degree such as the Ph.D., the M.D., etc. to believe that the degree confers with it omniscience and overall competence regardless of the nature of one's training. There is even a hierarchy among degrees, which is, at times, fostered by professional organizations and insurance companies. Witness the bizarre requirement—only recently eliminated in most states—regarding reimbursements of psychologists performing psychological evaluations. According to that requirement a psychologist to whom a patient was referred for consultation by a psychiatrist could only be reimbursed by an insurance company if his or her work was supervised by a physician. That physican could have been a urologist or a nose and throat specialist. It did not matter. As these artificial barriers to practice are gradually eliminated, and the awe that degrees inspire disappears, and as the competition becomes tougher, competence will become the crucial factor. The best group therapist will be the most successful.

2. *The therapist must believe in the efficacy of group therapy as a first class modality.* As stated at the beginning of this section, economic factors will be instrumental in making group therapy the trend of the future. It would be inadvisable for a therapist to engage in the practice of group therapy for only these reasons. If the therapist believes that group therapy is a second-rate modality of treatment, the belief will eventually be transmitted to the patients and a self-fulfilling prophecy will come true. If the therapist is not thoroughly convinced of the efficacy of group therapy, then he or she should limit his or her practice to that of the modality in which he or she believes.

3. *The therapist must always maintain the highest level of professional ethics.* Further discussion of the above guideline is,

of course, not needed. Not only will the private practice of an unethical therapist eventually flounder as his or her behavior becomes known in the community, but an unethical therapist should be prevented from practicing anywhere.

4. *The therapist should continue the practice of individual therapy and maintain a network of referrals.* One of the greatest difficulties encountered by therapists as they take their first steps toward building a practice of group therapy is how to form a group. It is indeed not easy to find six, seven, or more clients who are fairly compatible, willing to join a group, and can coordinate their schedules. There really is no one solution to the problem as reflected in my use of the word "should" rather than "must." I will share with the reader the ways that have worked well for me in overcoming that obstacle.

I have not discontinued the practice of individual therapy for two reasons. First, there is a great number of people who are reluctant initially to join a group and prefer to begin as individual patients and then join a group later. The second reason lies in my belief that the practice of a short-term individual therapy to be followed by participation in a group is sound, especially when the new patient comes in therapy while under considerable stress. A short-term period of individual therapy serves to alleviate some of the stress, enables the patient to define goals more clearly, and reduces the fears of groups. I do not, however, "trap" my patients. I make it clear to them that, after a period of individual therapy, I will broach again with them the possibility of joining a group. I make it no less clear that the final decision will be theirs and that I will abide by it, except in some rare cases when I might feel that further individual therapy could be harmful or useless. Approximately two-thirds of my patients choose to remain in individual therapy. The remaining third moves into a group and constitutes an important source of referral. It is interesting that, in the past 15 years, *not one* of them regretted the decision. Some new patients, of course, choose to join a group directly without the interim period of individual therapy.

I am not hesitant about advocating the use of group therapy and acquainting my professional colleagues with the nature of my work within the boundaries, of course, of professional ethics and good taste. I accept local invitations for workshops and speaking engagements to professional groups. Since I do believe in the usefulness of what I do, this is an easy and satisfying task. I have had several referrals from fellow professionals who have participated in my workshops and have heard me talk. Whenever I have such a referral, and of course with the client's permission, I religiously contact the referring sources to thank them and inform them of the disposition agreed upon. For awhile I struggled with the advisability of seeing in group people who were seen individually by another therapist. Several years ago, I decided to experiment with that model and found it very satisfactory. The only condition I place upon such an arrangement is to have the patient's blank permission to contact the other therapist should the need for a consultation arise. In the very rare cases where this became necessary, I talked with the client before and sometimes after talking to the other therapist.

5. *The therapist must be prepared.* I did not wait until my group therapy practice picked up to have an adequate comfortable group room where the clients felt at ease and safe from eavesdroppers. There is nothing inherently wrong with holding a group session anywhere. I believe, however, that clients who pay for a therapist's services directly (or even indirectly through a salary paid to the therapist by a publicly funded institution) have a right to comfort and privacy. It is up to them to forego that right and meet in a public square if they so desire. That right, however, must be afforded to them. Other aspects of the therapist's preparedness have been discussed at length in the chapter on logistics and will not be repeated here.

Finally, I have an important word of advice to the therapist in private practice who wishes to start a practice of group therapy: persevere, do not become discouraged. It takes a long time but it is worthwhile.

Chapter 7

CLINICAL ISSUES

I have singled out three clinical issues as deserving separate and additional treatment. I have done so for different reasons. I consider the issue of physical contact between therapist and client of importance because of its potential beneficial as well as harmful effects, because of the interest that it generates as well as the havoc that it can wreak upon the practice of psychotherapy and the profession of psychotherapist. In a preceding chapter, I had discussed it at length and suggested several principles to govern the use of physical contact in psychotherapy. In this chapter, I will present some empirical data to back these principles.

I have chosen to write about termination from group because of a personal interest in the matter. Finally, I have included the topic of the symbolic death of a group member because of the inherent danger in using such a technique unless it is clearly understood.

TOUCHING IN GROUP THERAPY

In 1969, the fall issue of *Psychotherapy: Theory, Research and Practice* contained a flurry of articles dealing with the issue of touching in psychotherapy. (Forer, 1969). These articles will not be discussed or summarized here except to point out that not only do opinions widely diverge, but that well-known, reputable therapists have, over the years, modified their attitudes and ways of thinking on the matter (Mintz, 1972). All these articles had one feature in common. Knowledgeable and sensitive as the expressed opinions were, they reflected the author's point of view. None of the writers had chosen to explore the opinions and points of view of the patients themselves.

Spurred by that realization, I mailed a questionnaire to 23 individual patients who had terminated therapy for at least six months but for no longer than one year and who had been in therapy for at least one year.* All the patients were women since no men met the time requirement. Since that endeavor could not be considered methodologically sound research, I had not submitted it for publication. I had, however, derived many learnings from it and I believe that, within the context of this chapter, these learnings may prove of interest and, although derived from patients in individual therapy, may be extrapolated to group therapy patients.

Method

A questionnaire was mailed to 23 patients and was accompanied by a covering explanatory letter and a self-addressed,

---

*It is interesting to note that my practice, at that time, was constituted almost entirely of female patients. Today, approximately, 45 percent of my patients are men. It is possible that this was a result of my working in a Community Mental Health Center, a tax-funded institution affording less privacy to privacy-conscious male patients. I believe, however, that this interesting and welcome change in client population is in major part due to the influence of the feminist movement. I have no doubt that it has liberated men from many cultural inhibitions around seeking psychotherapy.

stamped envelope. Participants were requested, of course, to maintain anonymity in their replies. The questionnaire had three parts. The first part attempted to tap the respondents' feelings and attitudes toward a physical contact. The second and third parts dealt with the fantasies of the clients and their perceived changes as a result of therapy. They will not be discussed here except to state with some satisfaction that eighteen of nineteen respondents felt that they had reached most of their goals in therapy. Part I of the questionnaire is reproduced below:

Questionnaire
Part I
Technique

Age: _____   Dates of Therapy
Sex: _____   From: _____ To: _____
Background: _____

Until recently, communication between therapist and client has traditionally been of a verbal nature. Comfort, reassurance, support, etc. was provided through words only.

Recently, some psychotherapists have advocated the use of nonverbal communication in addition to the verbal interaction. They feel that comfort or support can better (or equally well) be expressed by a gesture, a physical contact, a gentle touch at a moment of crisis or despair.

Both schools of thought present good theoretical and practical reasons for their positions. The purpose of this questionnaire is to find out the feelings and attitudes of the clients themselves regarding the above two questions.

While this is obviously quite difficult to do and will necessitate a great deal of remembering and introspecting, try to answer the following questions not as you feel now but as you would have felt, then, while you were in therapy.

Your help will be greatly appreciated:

1. If during therapy, at times when I was feeling particularly lonely or depressed—at a time of crisis or despair—my therapist had reached for me and touched me in some way, I

would have felt: PLEASE CHECK ONE OF EACH FIVE CHOICES:

   a. Very reassured _____
   b. Reassured _____
   c. No different _____
   d. Worried _____
   e. Very worried _____

I would also have felt:

   a. Very relaxed _____
   b. Relaxed _____
   c. No different _____
   d. Tense _____
   e. Very tense _____

I would also have felt:

   a. That he liked me a lot _____
   b. That he liked me _____
   c. That his feelings about me were neutral _____
   c. That he disliked me _____
   e. That he disliked me a lot _____

I also would have felt:

   a. That he trusted me a lot _____
   b. That he trusted me _____
   c. No different _____
   d. That he distrusted me _____
   e. That he distrusted me a lot _____

I also would have felt:

   a. Like a very worthy person _____
   b. Like a worthy person _____
   c. No different _____
   d. Like an unworthy person _____
   e. Like a very unworthy person _____

2. Please write in your own words (saying whatever you would like to say) what you think or feel about nonverbal communication in therapy; how could it have affected your own therapy and relationship with Dr. Naar, and how could it have affected your therapy and relationship with a different therapist.

Results

Two of the questionnaires were returned, the addressees having moved without leaving a forwarding address. Nineteen of the remaining twenty-one clients answered and their answers are summarized below.

Question 1. If during therapy, at times when I was feeling particularly lonely and depressed—at a moment of crisis or despair—my therapist had reached for me and touched me in some way, I would have felt: PLEASE CHECK ONE OF EACH FIVE CHOICES:

	Choices	Number of Responses
a.	Very reassured	3
b.	Reassured	10
c.	No difference	4
d.	Worried	0
e.	Very worried	2
a.	Very relaxed	1
b.	Relaxed	11
c.	No different	0
d.	Tense	5
e.	Very tense	2
a.	That he liked me a lot	6
b.	That he liked me	10
c.	That his feelings about me were neutral	3
d.	That he disliked me	0
e.	That he disliked me a lot	0

a.	That he trusted me a lot	2
b.	That he trusted me	10
c.	No different	7
d.	That he distrusted me	0
e.	That he distrusted me a lot	0
a.	Like a very worthy person	3
b.	Like a worthy person	9
c.	No different	6
d.	Like an unworthy person	1
e.	Like a very unworthy person	0

There was a total of 65 positive, 20 neutral, and 10 negative responses.

The answers to the second question, however, were puzzling. All nineteen respondents, without exception, agreed that a physical contact as described in the questionnaire, would be helpful; yet, in discussing their own therapy, they split in two groups. The first half stated that had I resorted to a physical gesture, our relationship and the therapeutic process would have been damaged. The other half wrote that both the relationship and the therapeutic process were enhanced because I had used physical contact. Two sample comments are quoted below:

> This is a difficult question. I feel so much more secure now than I did at the time of my therapy. As I think about the possibilities of nonverbal communication for others, it seems as though it would be an invaluable way of relaying the trust and true concern of the therapist for the patient. I do, however, think that in my case it would have injured my relationship with Dr. Naar. During that time I was very insecure and my feelings for Dr. Naar were not clear. I wanted to be very important to him. He gave me that feeling without reaching for me or touching me. A touch would have confused me or given me doubts about his sincerity. He worked much longer and harder with words and

kindness. This effort convinced me that I must be a person worthy of this labor. I am a woman. If my therapist had been a woman (and if I liked her) a touch would have been a reassuring experience.

> The nonverbal communication used by Dr. Naar was often the most meaningful part of my sessions with him. His facial expression of deep concern immediately made me feel comfortable. His eyes have a way of saying everything from "You can trust me" to "I think you are a good person" to "I am puzzled by what you say." On several occasions when I became tearful and was feeling tremendous emotional pain in expressing some very deep thoughts, Dr. Naar drew his chair closer to me and held my hand. It was a much longed for experience, but one I had never had except from my husband. It was something I had always wanted from a parent figure and never got. For the first time in my life this physical reassurance and closeness made me feel like it was OK to cry and that, in the process, I wasn't behaving like a child. Termination was an extremely difficult time for me because I didn't want to let go of what I felt had become a deeply meaningful relationship, not only for me but also for Dr. Naar. He really made me feel that he enjoyed seeing me as much as I enjoyed seeing him and that both of us were learning through the encounter. On our final meeting he gave me a handshake and a hug which I'll never forget because it said without words that he was sharing in the excitement of my changing self and that he would always be there if I felt the need to come back.

The puzzle was somewhat clarified when I checked the periods during which the respondents had been in therapy. Approximately one-half the respondents had been in therapy before my active involvement with groups. The opinions and feelings of that first half were similar to the first comment quoted above. During that period of my professional life, I considered even a handshake to be totally inappropriate. The second half of the respondents had come into therapy after I had begun to attend groups as a member. My attitude toward touching was beginning to change both toward men and women. Having been raised in a Mediterranean country where physical contact was part of everyday life, it was easy to revert to old ways of communicating. The way in which my experiences affected the answers of my patients will be discussed below.

Discussion

The overwhelming positive answers to the first question clearly suggest that clients may not have the same aversion as therapists to a gesture of friendship and/or support. In fact, the dogmatic attitude of some therapists in their blank indictment of any kind of physical contact may, indeed, represent their own fear and discomfort rationalized under the guise of concern for their patients.

The responses to the second item of my questionnaire strongly imply that my attitudes were sensed by and affected my clients. During the years when I considered touching an absolute taboo, my clients felt that such an experience would be damaging to our relationship but would be beneficial to other people. When I felt more comfortable with this mode of communication, my clients felt that it had been of help to them.

While these modest empirical findings do not have the weight of well-controlled research, they are sufficient to reinforce my belief in the soundness of the guidelines that I had outlined in Chapter 4 regarding physical contact in therapy. These guidelines are repeated below and somewhat expanded upon:

1. Physical gestures of support and affection are desirable and should be encouraged. Indeed, they represent an important mode of communication of which people should not be deprived.
2. Such expressions should be limited in scope. More extensive physical contact could easily become erotic and be used for the sexual gratification of the giver

rather than being an expression of support and/or affection for the recipient. Erotic physical contacts are seen as *unequivocally unethical behavior* on the part of the therapist.

3. Physical (as well as verbal) expressions of support and/ or affection should be used only when they are meant and never in a ritualistic, mechanical, or manipulative fashion.

4. The group leader must be comfortable with physical contact. Discomfort at touching is discernible, and the gesture of support may lose its significance and even become damaging.

5. Because of the importance that he or she acquires for group members, the leader will use physical expressions of support and affection sparingly and never preempt group members who are willing and able to offer the same kind of support and affection to the person in need.

TERMINATION FROM GROUP

In describing the therapist's feelings toward a member's termination, I would like to talk only about myself because these are very personal feelings. I suspect, however, that my feelings are, in one way or another, shared by most of my colleagues.

The average stay of members in my group is approximately two years. During that time I become attached to them. When they terminate, I experience many different, conflicting feelings. I feel a lot of professional pride and satisfaction. I like to believe that a successful termination is due in part to the client's efforts and motivation but also to my work and skills. A successful termination validates me as a professional person. I also experience much joy at seeing a person I like being happier, more contented, free from the ghosts of the past and able to enjoy life and interpersonal relationships more fully. At the same time, however, I feel a sense of loss, a sadness made partly of the knowledge that I will not see again a person I care for and partly of the less rational feeling that, in some way, I am left behind and, partly of a slight twinge of worry at how well they will do on their own. With much less intensity, every time a member graduates, I feel the way my wife and I did when our son went to college. I recognize in myself that tendency to be overprotective and try to curb it and even warn my clients to be on the lookout for it.

From a client's point of view, the feelings are equally ambivalent and, often, more complex. As in any intense inter-personal relationship, participation in a group experience is a source of both joy and pain. Many new learnings are acquired, many old habits discarded. To grow is challenging and exciting but it also hurts; because of the pain involved in the process, many members tend to want to terminate prematurely. Some-times, the decision to terminate hides anger at the group which, for one reason or another cannot meet the person's need. At other times, it is the sign of an impasse. The member feels stuck and chooses withdrawal as the easiest way to solve the dilemma. Often the impasse simply means that the client has reached the point where he or she really feels the need to share but has not overcome the fear of exposure. To put it in different terms, the tendency toward sharing and the tendency toward not exposing oneself are of equal strengths (Dollard & Miller, 1950). In spite of the member's denials, it is easy to determine whether the termination is legitimate or premature. The best criterion is the reaction of the group. If the pain, joy, as well as anxiety ex-pressed by the group are spontaneous and genuine, then the termination is legitimate. If the group's reaction is forced and superficial then the termination is not legitimate. I put no pres-sure upon group members to stay except to request that mem-bers who wish to terminate share and discuss their decision with the group one week before termination.

On the other hand, if it is quite obvious that the decision is premature, it is incumbent both upon the group and the group leader to help the terminating member explore the conflict further and, if possible, solve it. This is illustrated in the following vignettes:

> Sally, a 45-year-old woman, had been in a group for approximately a year. She was a warm, gentle person, very nurturant and sensitive to the needs of others. Sally: It is now time for me to terminate. I have been here for over a year and you have all been very wonderful to me. I really appreciate everything that you have done for me and I feel a lot better. I just think it's time to terminate.
>
> The group had a somewhat superficial interaction, congratulating Sally and expressing some ambivalence at letting her go.
>
> Therapist: Sally, I would like you to do something. Could you imagine that you are at home and you are writing a letter to the group, stating your reasons for leaving.
> Sally: O.K. Dear Group: I feel that I have reached a point in the group beyond which I cannot go. You have given me much and I appreciate it, but I do feel that I must now be on my own and be less dependent. I feel strong enough that I can do it. I hope the best for you and hope to see you again from time to time. Love, Sally.
> Therapist: Now, Sally I would like you to move over to that pillow. Imagine that you are the group. You have received Sally's letter. How would you answer it?
> Sally: O.K. I would say . . . Dear Sally: We received your letter and read it with mixed feelings. We are happy to see that you have achieved your goals, but we are sorry to see you go. We'll miss you. We could always turn to you and rely on you. You were always there to support us and give us help when we needed it.
> Therapist: Now answer as yourself.
> Sally: I know. I have given you much help, and sometimes I feel . . . I feel (sigh) I feel (tears come to her eyes) that nobody really

cares. Nobody reciprocates. It is as if I cannot turn to anyone for help. I get very tired sometimes.

Therapist: Now change seats and be the group.

Sally (as group): You never told us. We would have helped you but you always seemed so strong. Why didn't you say something?

Sally (as Sally): I never could. It was the same thing when I was a child. I was always the one to take care of my younger sisters. Always. Nobody ever would take care of me. I was always strong. Goddammit. It's always been like that.

The group then dealt with Sally's feelings, shared their own opinions that had been accurately reflected by Sally, and, as a result, she remained in the group for another year.

Joe was a somewhat withdrawn, intellectual person who shared very little of himself and had never been able to explain what he was doing in the group. Yet, he never missed a session and was always on time. One evening he abruptly stated that he had decided not to come back. The group refused to take his statement at face value. Instead, they gathered around him and they talked to him very softly, very gently. I was so moved by that display of sensitivity that its impact lingered long after the group left, and I neglected to take notes after the group's departure. I do not know what the group told Joe. All I remember is that Joe's chest began to heave, his lower lip to quiver, and he burst into tears. When Joe left the group two years later, it was a joyous celebration.

But the day comes, of course, when termination is authentic. It is a time to go and be on one's own. When this time arrives, the group and the leader have to deal with that process. The feelings of the leader were discussed earlier from a rather personal point of view. The feelings of those who stay behind have two components; for example, they are a reaction to the present happening, that is the joy to see a close friend progress, strike out on one's own, and the resentment at being left behind, the pain and sadness of the loss. These feelings, however, are more than just a reaction to the present happening; they are also tied to the past, to all the memories, pain, sadness of past separations, and reactivated by the member's termination. I believe that the latter component is better dealt with in subsequent sessions. I prefer to use the last session to deal only with the group's reaction to the present happening and also with the feelings of the member who leaves. I do so within the context of the three goals that I believe one should attempt to reach at termination. One of these goals is to bring to closure whatever unfinished business may still remain between the person who leaves and those who are left behind, and residual feelings of affection or anger felt at one time or another in the group and not expressed for a number of reasons. The second goal is to reinforce the learning that has occurred and to reverbalize the insights acquired during the stay in the group. Third, it is important that the terminating group member be able and have the opportunity to express both the sadness and joy of leaving as well as the opportunity to experience the resentment and affection of the group.

In order to reach these goals, I have devised a fairly simple exercise that I have called *currents*. I have called it *currents* because the movement of the group members during the exercise are reminiscent of sea currents. Currents, which is described below, make use of motion, verbal interactions, and space. Usually the group members are sitting on the floor and the instructions to the group are as follows:

> We have all been together over a long period. During this time, many things happened involving Anna (the terminating group member) and the rest of us. Some of these things may stick out in our memory as landmarks in our relationship. What I would like us to do is take some time and meander through our memories. Go back over the time which we have all spent together. Remember things that happened and, as you do, verbalize your memory, put it into words, and remember how you felt at the time this happened. If, at that time, you felt angry at Anna, or distant from her, then move into the room at a distance that would indicate the nature and the intensity of the feelings you

experienced then. If, on the other hand, the feelings were feelings of affection, of closeness, then again move closer to her, again at a distance that would indicate the intensity and the nature of what you felt then. Anna, of course, will participate in the exercise and remember events and memories that have involved her with the rest of the group members.

A TERMINATION SESSION

Selma: I feel so sad at your leaving now because I love you so much, and yet I am so happy for you. I remember our first encounter. I screamed at you and was so angry with you. But instead of being afraid of me and shutting up, you screamed back at me, and that frightened me so much. It was the first time in my life that someone had stood up to me and was not cowed by my anger. I didn't know how to take that. I was so scared; and later, it was perhaps one of the best things that happened to me. I realized that I was not all powerful nor was I destructive. At that moment, however, I felt very angry and afraid of you.

(At that, Selma moves away from Anna and goes to the other end of the room.)

Anna (to Group Leader): I remember, Ray, the time when I was crying so hard, feeling so miserable, and saying that nobody liked me and nobody cared for me. And you turned to me and you sounded very cold when you said "Has it ever occurred to you that maybe you are the one who likes no one, who does not care?" At that time, this really devastated me, coming from you because for all the years that I've known you, you have always been so caring and so warm and I just hated your guts for saying this. But when I went home that night, I thought about it and realized that you were right, that I was doing this, and that was a turning point in my life, both in the group and outside the group. At the time it happened, however, I really wanted to kill you.

(Anna moved away from the Leader.)

John: I remember the time I played your father. You seemed so fragile and so unhappy, and yet so willing to fight. I felt so close to you and I wanted to tell you then, but things were happening too fast, and then when the psychodrama was over, I was feeling too many other things.

(John moves quite close to Anna.)

Herb: You know, so many times I came into the group feeling low and down, and you would look up and smile at me and you have a beautiful smile and especially those times when I had disagreements with my daughter, whom I love so much, and you're about her age, and your smiling at me was almost like having another daughter being gentle with me. And I just love you for it.

(And he, also, moves close to Anna.)

As memories continue to be brought from the past into the present, feelings reexperienced, verbalized, a sense of closure begins to be felt. Over time, I became aware of an interesting phenomenon. Unexpressed feelings of hostility and anger are verbalized first, probably because of the safety felt by the fact that they belong to the past and they can now be expressed and verbalized with the shared knowledge that the two involved members now do love each other; there is no fear of rejection or retaliation. Feelings of love and affection are left for the end, and the group ends up in a very tight cluster around the terminating member. Usually, at that time, a silence occurs, there is a sense of fulfillment, completeness. And, usually, it is followed by physical demonstrations of affection: hugging, shaking hands and inquiries into plans for the future. By that time, the session is usually over.

THE DEATH SCENE

My reasons for treating the "death scene" separately are somewhat different. Indeed, the opportunities for using that technique are rare. On the other hand, it is quite powerful and, since it is mentioned twice in this book, it is appropriate to discuss it further and point out some very real dangers inherent in its use and the conditions under which it may be used.

The times when I use the death scene are limited. I use it only when the person having suicidal fantasies is motivated by extreme loneliness, anger at one's environment (In such cases killing oneself is a way of punishing the environment.); and a denial and escape of one's despair.

In the case of the priest whose death fantasy was enacted, his make-believe death helped to put him in touch with the very real affection that group members felt for him. In the case of Nancy, the 42-year-old woman threatened with a double mastectomy, no amount of encouragement and/or advice helped, until her symbolic death enabled her to feel her total, utter despair.

In the rare cases where the death scene is used, the following prerequisites are necessary and the following cautions should be taken:

1. The therapist must be *thoroughly* trained in personality, human behavior and psychopathology.
2. The therapist must be thoroughly trained in psychodrama.
3. The therapist must have worked with that particular group long enough to be able to predict group members' reactions.
4. The therapist must be *thoroughly* familiar with the background, past experiences, and ego strength of the member whose death is enacted. Only well-integrated people should be asked to go through that experience.
5. The therapist will *never* suggest, allow anyone to suggest or encourage the group member to define specific ways in which death will occur.*

*For further discussion of the death scene see Siroka (1968).

SUMMARY

This chapter dealt with the requirements and qualifications for leading a group, and discussed three clinical issues of importance.

The Group Leader. Among the factors discussed were

I. The Leader's Personality. It should be characterized by

1. *Acceptance*
2. *The awareness of one's needs and the ability to differentiate them from the needs of others.*
3. *The awareness of one's impact upon group members.*
4. *Effective ways of dealing with one's prejudices.*

II. The Leader's Training. AGPA guidelines and ASGPP requirements were discussed. A tri-level model of training and practice was suggested.

III. The Leader's Ethics. The following guidelines were offered to supplement existing codes of conduct:

1. *The therapist will never knowingly harm group members.*
2. *The therapist will never use group members for self-gratification.*
3. *The therapist will maintain himself/herself in good physical, psychological and emotional condition.*
4. *The therapist will establish a contract clearly and live up to the terms of that contract.*

IV. Starting and maintaining a private practice. The following suggestions were offered:

1. *The therapist must be thoroughly trained and competent in at least one approach to group therapy.*
2. *The therapist must believe in the efficacy of group therapy as a first class modality.*
3. *The therapist must always maintain the highest levels of professional ethics.*
4. *The therapist should continue the practice of individual therapy and maintain a network of referrals.*
5. *The therapist must be logistically prepared.*

Clinical issues. The following issues were discussed:

I. Touching in group therapy. Some empirical data was presented and its significance discussed.

II. Termination. The meaning of premature termination was discussed and a way of handling genuine termination was presented.

III. The death scene. A rationale for the death scene and contra-indications to its use were discussed.

Addendum

ELEMENTS OF PSYCHODRAMA

Psychodrama, of course, is the creation of Jacob Levy Moreno. Much has been written about him and, not being privy to factual or anecdotal information that has not already been printed, I only wish here to acknowledge a debt of gratitude to the man who, as he once told Freud, "gave people the courage to dream again."* Larger than life, he dominated the field of psychodrama and group therapy for half a century and, among those who knew him or about him his name became synonymous with spontaneity, creativity, and love.

I remember fondly my first and only encounter with Moreno several years before his death. I was accompanied by a good friend who had been his student for many years. Moreno was sitting in the lobby of the hotel where the yearly convention of the American Society for Group Psychotherapy and Psychodrama was being held. By some extraordinary set of circumstances, he was alone. My friend introduced us and all I could

*Moreno, Z. Personal communication.

say was "Dr. Moreno, what do you tell a legend when you see one?" He looked at me with a twinkle in his eyes, opened his arms, and replied "You say, I love you!" The man was in these words. To be called a legend was his due and he accepted it graciously and without protest. At the same time, however, he offered his love in exchange.

At times, I have felt a sense of loss and sorrow at not having been trained by Moreno; at times, I have felt rather fortunate. Indeed, it is hard to step from under the shadow of giants. It is not easy to strike on one's own, to deviate, to change when one has been the disciple of a Moreno or a Freud. I believe that I have, somewhat, deviated, and my understanding and practice of psychodrama is not always that of Moreno or of his closer followers. While I stand by my deviations, I wish to state how indebted I feel to the man whose life, work, as well as death, I have profoundly admired, and sometimes envied.

Psychodrama: A Theory or a Set of Techniques

To Moreno, psychodrama was a way of life. It was not a set of structured techniques to be used as a therapeutic modality. It was built upon complex, theoretical underpinnings that could be conceived as, and indeed were, not only a theory of personality and behavior, but also a philosophical approach to life (Moreno, 1964).

I prefer to look at psychodrama as a set of techniques but of such elegance, such flexibility that it can be used within any kind of theoretical framework. For example, its emphasis on action and on the here-and-now renders psychodrama particularly amenable to use within a Gestalt framework.* The protagonist can come in touch with successively emerging emo-

---

*Indeed, many of the techniques used by Gestalt therapists and encounter group leaders were borrowed from psychodrama (Perls, 1973; Shaffer & Galinsky, 1974).

tional states and is able to put closure to unfinished past events in one's life.

> Judith, a Catholic sister, was a member of a group of eight sisters which met on a weekly basis for approximately two years. Judith had been raised by extremely rejecting and ungiving parents and, several months before the group terminated, Judith talked about her father. For the first time she was able to ventilate anger at him. This very unusual behavior on her part was reinforced by other members of the group. Approximately an hour after the group had left, there was a knock at my office door. Judith, trembling and white as a sheet, was standing on the threshold. I helped her in and she explained that while she was expressing anger at her father with the group, he was dying (in fact, had died) of a sudden heart attack in the Emergency Room located in another part of the hospital.
>
> In an understandable illustration of parataxic thinking, Judith held herself responsible for her father's death. She became obsessed with his memory, dreamed of him every night, and thought of him constantly during the day. She refused to talk about her experiences with him, however, except to point out that he was a good man and that she had been a terrible daughter for having accused him and been angry at him. Approximately eight months later, she stated brusquely that she could stand this no longer, that she realized that her father was not what she pretended and that she wanted to get rid of that unbearable obsession. The drama began with a dialogue between Judith and her father. At the beginning of the interaction, Judith was subdued and talked in a very soft voice, sounding apologetic and fearful. As the exchange continued, however, Judith's anger began to mount. Using the "shut-up" technique developed by Sacks (1976) that essentially consists of initially thwarting the patient's efforts at expressing his or her feelings and reinforcing increments of anger, the person playing the part of Judith's father was successful in helping Judith become extremely angry. Suddenly, she literally exploded and, screaming at the top of her lungs, spewed forth a torrent of accusations and abuse, at last telling her father all the things that she had wanted but been afraid to tell him throughout her life: all the anger, all the hate, all the rejection, the hurts for which he had been responsible for in the past. When she was finally exhausted, her father, in the

drama became a reformed parent (Sachs, 1970),* changed his attitude and softly, gently stated that "maybe she was right and truly he wanted to, at last, hear her." Then, somewhat wistfully and sadly, she spent many minutes sharing with him, this time without anger, the hurt that he had caused her, the pain, the fear, the loneliness, the times when she would do anything to get his attention and would never get it. When she was finished, she was sobbing, again an emotional manifestation extremely rare in her. In the darkness, she embraced her father and, to my question, replied that it was now all right for him to die and leave. Several weeks later, Judith sent me a note, excerpts of which are quoted below:*

> He (the father) was with me all the time, like haunting me. I couldn't get away from him. In the psychodrama, for the first time in my life, what I was feeling and what I was saying were together. For the first time I was feeling anger and expressing it verbally. This may not seem like much but to me it was one of the greatest experiences of my life. Before that day, the only feeling I had for my father was a strong hatred. Only after expressing my anger did I not only realize I loved him, but I also felt that love . . .

With its infinite possibilities, transcending time and space, psychodrama is admirably suited for use within a psychoanalytic framework. Insight into introjection of parental values and attitudes as well as into transferences can be achieved and, sometimes, dealt with as illustrated in the following anecdote.

> Ethel, a 45-year-old successful businesswoman, was sharing with the group her ambivalent feelings about her best friend, a woman

*The reformed auxiliary ego (i.e., reformed parent) is specially conceived to bring into awareness both repressed love and repressed needs for love (Sachs, 1970). What the technique entails has been essentially described above.

*For a more detailed description of Judith's case, see Naar (1979). I wish to thank the editor of *Psychotherapy Theory, Research and Practice* for his gracious permission to quote extensively from the article.

her age with a club foot who walked assisted by a cane and with great difficulty. She stated "At times, I feel as if she manipulates me and uses me as a servant. I have to take her places, buy her groceries, run her errands. Goddamn it! Half those things she can do by herself. When I tell her to get lost, she looks so lost, and miserable that I can't stand it and I say 'OK, OK' because basically I care for her very much." At my suggestion, a member of the group played the part of Ethel's friend and the subtle manipulation was evident and amusing. Through the use of a soliloquy and a double (see following section for a definition of these terms), Ethel explored the nature of her emotional reactions to her friend's manipulations. At one point, she stated "I feel just like a teenager when I would disobey my mother. She would never punish me or threaten me. She would simply die of a heart attack. She has been dying of a heart attack for the past forty years. She is now 79." At that point, a group member volunteered to play the part of Ethel's mother. Ethel and her mother had quite a lively exchange, Ethel telling her mother exactly what she thought of her heart attacks and her manipulation. Buoyed by her encounter with her mother, Ethel turned to her girlfriend and in affectionate, but very firm terms, laid down guidelines for a healthier, future relationship. This was reinforced by the group, and Ethel stated that, upon her return home, she would immediately call her friend and put into practice what she had rehearsed during the psychodrama.

A final, rather amusing, example will illustrate how psychodramatic techniques can fit learning theory concepts and can be used by behavior therapists.

Marcia, an attractive and vivacious woman in her early forties, was very upset as she entered the group room. She explained that, as she was about to back into a parking space in a busy street, an old lady in a big car had driven into it. Marcia, flustered and angry, but afraid of a confrontation, drove away. We reenacted the scene. Two chairs became the car, one of the group members became the old lady and Marcia was helped to confront her and express her indignation and anger. A good time was had by all. Several months later, Marcia came into the group roaring with laughter and this is what she said: "Well, you won't believe this, but there I was on Murray Avenue, again ready to back into that space and bingo! she drives into it. Now, I don't know whether it was the same old lady but didn't give a shit. For a second there, I had almost like the impulse to drive away, then thought the hell with it. I double parked, went to the old lady's car and, boy did I let her have it! I tell you; I was proud of myself. Then, as I was about to walk away, she leans over from her window, and, without cracking a smile, she says 'What did you say? I am deaf. I can't hear a thing'."

Glossary and Techniques

It is obvious from the few illustrations already presented that awareness, closure, and rehearsal of new behaviors can be met through the use of psychodrama alone. An excellent case can be made for using psychodrama as the sole modality in groups and for bothering minimally with the nature of the process. I prefer not to do so and my reasons, which could legitimately be disputed, are described below.

First, because of its structure and the fact that much of the responsibility for the action is borne by the director, psychodrama does away with the discomfort and anxiety experienced in interpersonal encounters. Discomfort and anxiety are somewhat inadequate words to describe what one feels in a group with new people. It is not just the threat of a new situation, it is not an objective fear caused by a danger that can be pinpointed, fought, or avoided; it is a deeper feeling that puts one directly in touch with the vulnerability of one's total being. It can be argued that it is not necessary to feel that way if open communication can be achieved without it. It is indeed a defensible point, but one with which I do not agree. Not every person we enter in contact with has had the opportunity to participate in a group encounter, and it is good, perhaps essential, that those of us who have, can understand and appreciate the feeling of vulnerability of those we come in contact with when they are called upon to share their world and reveal themselves.

A similar question often arises as to whether a warm-up (the nature of the warm-up will be described later) is useful in beginning a session. There is no doubt that the use of a warm-up in order to initiate a group session has many advantages. It cuts through the initial anxiety and silence; it quickly stimulates people and puts them in touch with their feelings; it promotes cohesiveness and openness, and of course, leads to the selection of a protagonist. The warm-up, however, takes away from group participants the opportunity to experience what it feels like to come face to face with the possibility that one will open oneself up and share that unprotected self honestly with other people. It is my belief that the pain and fear have to be experienced.

Second, because of psychodrama's focus on the protagonist, intragroup tensions become less evident. There is, sometimes, a tendency among members of psychodrama groups to still disagreements or negative feelings toward each other in order not to interrupt the flow of protagonist-centered action. These unspoken tensions may interfere with the growth of spontaneity and, occasionally, be responsible for the break-up of a group. An unstructured interaction among group members permits these tensions to emerge before they reach the danger point. Psychodramatic interventions may, then, be quite helpful in alleviating them.

Third, I also believe that a group that does not use psychodrama as the exclusive modality enables its members not only to shed their defenses as they interact with each other but also to gain insight into those defenses and into what they do in order to isolate themselves.

There is no doubt that even the above shortcomings could be overcome through the use of psychodrama alone. The director, however, would have to be extremely skilled. This kind of skill takes many years to acquire and may not be available to many therapists. For these reasons I prefer to use psychodrama only when dealing with the content of the communication and in order to help group members solve specific problems.

I would like to make one additional point. Psychodramatic interventions are powerful tools. It is not sufficient that the user be well-versed in the use of the techniques. He or she must also be steeped in a thorough knowledge of human behavior, personality, laws of learning, and psychopathology. While some techniques may be used in an exploratory fashion, the therapist must be aware of the impact of psychodramatic interventions, be able to set goals, make predictions, and shift aim if the original hypotheses are not confirmed. It is not essential that the therapist (or Director) be guided by the theoretical concepts developed by Moreno or work within some other traditional and well accepted theoretical framework. It is important, however, that he or she work within a logically consistent theory of personality and behavior that is connected to empirical data (Hall & Lindzey, 1957).

It is assumed that the motivated reader seeking training in psychodrama will also have the generic training enabling him or her to operate within such a theoretical framework. No attempt will, therefore, be made here to discuss contemporary theories of personality.

As implied above, it is my preference to intervene in a psychodramatic fashion whenever a group member struggles with an issue that cannot be resolved with the aid of the group alone. Sometimes, the intervention can be brief, almost surgical in nature as will be illustrated later; at other times, it may consist of a longer, more involved psychodrama. Occasionally, I proceed with a more classical approach without waiting for a specific issue or problem to be brought up. By a "more classical approach," I mean beginning with a warm-up leading to the choice of a protagonist, etc. The reasons militating for a brief or more involved intervention or for a more classical approach will be discussed later in this chapter. At this point, the reader will be acquainted with some of the terminology and key concepts. Because the purpose of this addendum is only to acquaint the reader with psychodrama and not to train psychodramatists, the description and discussion of these concepts will be sketchy. At the end of the chapter, however, a list of relevant readings will be provided for the reader who wishes to explore psychodramatic theory and techniques in greater depth.*

A Psychodrama

A classical psychodrama consists generally of three stages: the warm-up, the drama and the sharing phase. Some of the other concepts that will be described below include the protagonist, the auxiliary egos, the double, the soliloquy, and the role reversal.

THE WARM-UP.   The warm-up is a group exercise not unlike some of the group games popularized by the encounter movement. There are, of course, many kinds of warm-ups, verbal, nonverbal, cluster warm-ups, etc. The purpose of a warm-up exercise, as well as some of its advantages were briefly discussed earlier. As its title implies, the warm-up primes the group for action and quickly puts members in touch with their feelings. It does away with the painful initial silence and discomfort, quickly builds group cohesiveness and leads to the choice of a protagonist. A very moving warm-up, demonstrated for the first time in my presence by James Sacks is described below.*

> Director to Group: We often talk about "unfinished businesses" in people's lives. For me, "unfinished businesses" refer to all the times in my life when I could have said something but did not, I could have done something but did not. It means the unexpressed feelings, the missed opportunities and most always, it is in relation to another person. We all have "unfinished businesses" in our lives. I would like each of you to remember one

*I wish to thank Valerie J. Greer and James M. Sachs for having allowed me to sample from their very exhaustive *Bibliography of Psychodrama.*

*Sacks, James, Personal communication 1968. See also Lippitt, R., The auxiliary chair technique. Complete reference is cited in the suggested readings.

unfinished business, and in your fantasy, place the person to whom the unfinished business relates on this empty chair. Then, we'll go around the circle and share with each other whatever we feel comfortable in sharing and no more.

The above instructions usually evoke a considerable amount of poignant memories. Some typical responses are:

I wish I could have told my grandparent how much I loved him/her before he/she died.

My unfinished business is with a girlfriend I had. She broke up our relationship for no reason and I never told her how I felt about it.

I'll never forget my third grade teacher. She gave me more self-confidence than any other person in my life. I wish I knew where she was so I could tell her that I've done well.

THE PROTAGONIST.   As stated above, the warm-up leads to the choice of a protagonist. The protagonist is the center figure of the drama, the person around whom all the action unfolds. In ongoing groups, selecting a protagonist presents no difficulty. The group member with an issue that the group cannot help in solving becomes the *de facto* protagonist. In workshops of brief duration, choosing a protagonist becomes a more delicate matter. The choice is dictated by a number of considerations, not the least of which is the time available to the Director. If the group does not meet again, it is incumbent upon the Director to see to it that the protagonist reaches some kind of closure, of conflict resolution. This may not always be possible during the time allotted for the workshop. The extent to which the protagonist is in touch with his or her feelings and the conflict lends itself to psychodramatic interventions,* the protagonist's motivation are additional criteria affecting the Director's choice. One must also remember that psychodrama is a very

---

*Theoretically, all situations are amenable to psychodramatic handling. There are, however, some rare exceptions. One such set of circumstances may involve actions committed by the protagonist in the past but still subject to criminal prosecution. In a workshop of brief duration, it may not be possible to deal with the conflict which such an occurrence may arouse among group members.

seductive modality and that a group member may be trapped into becoming a protagonist then, later, feel that his or her privacy was violated. The Director must be certain that the protagonist is really willing to work and is not subtly coerced into an activity for which he or she is not ready. On the other hand, many seemingly reluctant protagonists simply desire some encouragement. A trained Director must be able to discern the member who wishes to be seduced into becoming the focus of the action from the one who truly does not want to come forth. The privacy and wishes of the latter must always be respected.

THE SOLILOQUY.   The soliloquy is, exactly, what the name implies. The protagonist (or any other member of the drama) is asked to soliloquize, i.e., talk to him- or herself, to verbalize thoughts and feelings. Usually the protagonist is asked to imagine himself or herself in the place where, as a child, (or even as an adolescent or adult) he or she would feel safe and use as a retreat. At other times, the protagonist may be asked to stop an ongoing interaction and go into a soliloquy as illustrated in the brief example that follows.

> Protagonist: (to older brother) You never paid any attention to me. I was nonexistent for you. "Shithead," that's what you would call me and you never let me play with any of your friends.
> Older brother: My friends were all I had, shithead, and I wasn't about to let you take them away from me as you did Mom and Dad. Did it ever occur to you that, from the day you were born, I no longer mattered. It was Jason here, Jason there. Take care of Jason. Well, piss on Jason. At least he wasn't about to take my friends.
> Director: (to protagonist) Jason, I want you to go into a soliloquy about what just happened.
> Protagonist: (soliloquizing) Well, he may have a point there; come to think of it, I would always run to Mom when I wanted to get at him. I never knew he felt as strongly about it. Really, I think he should work it out with Dad and Mom. But, it bothers me . . . it really does . . . he hates me.

> Protagonist: (to brother) You know I care for you . . . I really . . . well, it was partly my fault . . .

As is true of all psychodramatic interventions, the soliloquy may serve a multiplicity of purposes. In the example described above, the soliloquy helped the protagonist distance himself from the heat of the interaction, see the situation in a somewhat more objective manner, and even get in touch with some tender feelings toward his brother. At other times, the soliloquy helps the protagonist in formulating the problem more clearly and provides the Director with additional data necessary to direct the drama.

AUXILIARY EGOS.   All participants in the drama, with the exception, of course, of the protagonist are called auxiliary egos. Their function is to help expand the protagonist's intellectual and affective awareness. It is also to help the protagonist develop new behavioral ways of coping with old and new situations.

THE DOUBLE.   One auxiliary ego serves a very special function and is called the double. The most important function of the double is to expand the protagonist's awareness. The double "becomes" the protagonist and talks "as if" he or she were the protagonist whenever the double feels that the protagonist is not completely in touch with or not quite able to verbalize feelings and ideas. There are many different ways to double, and the interested reader may refer to the bibliography at the end of this addendum. Some fairly elementary doubling techniques will be described below. The double usually stands to the right or left of the protagonist, close enough to be able to observe the protagonist's facial expression but not so close as to inhibit the protagonist by an intrusive presence. It is not absolutely necessary that the double assume the same position as the protagonist. Assuming the same position helps, however, in that it provides the double with additional kinesthetic cues to the protagonist's inner world. Interpreting is a doubling technique that one should refrain from. The reasons for avoiding interpretations in doubling are essentially the same militating against interpretations in group process. These reasons were discussed at length in a preceding chapter and will not be repeated here. It is also important that the protagonist feel free to contradict the double when the double is not "tuned in." This should be made clear to both protagonist and double.

Doubling as a Client-Centered Reflection of Feelings

> Protagonist: I went to pick her up and, well, . . . she told me to kiss off. Well, that's the way it goes. I didn't know what to do . . . and . . .
> Double: It felt awkward . . . felt more than awkward . . . it hurt . . .
> Protagonist: Yes, it did . . . right then and there I felt like bursting into tears.

Doubling as a Matching of Words, Feelings, and Tone of Voice

> Protagonist (in a matter of fact tone of voice): So, my little girl is not so little anymore. She got married and left home.
> Double (in a very soft tone of voice): She left home.
> Protagonist: (Nods with tears in her eyes).

Doubling as Incomplete Sentences

> Protagonist: What I told him was that I was sorry and that I would be more careful next time.
> Double: What I wanted to tell him was . . .
> Protagonist: What I really wanted to tell him was "Fuck off, you big tub of lard."

ROLE REVERSAL   The role reversal is a procedure according to which two protagonists in a drama (usually the protagonist and an auxiliary ego) reverse roles and assume each other's identity. The role reversal may be very brief or may last for several minutes. As usual, a role reversal may serve many purposes, some of which are described below:

A Role Reversal Helps the Auxiliary Ego become Acquainted with his or her Role. The protagonist is asked to play the part of the person to be depicted by the auxiliary ego.
A Role Reversal Helps an Individual Reincorporate One's Projections.

> Protagonist: In our fifteen years of married life, you never once trusted me.
> Director: Please, reverse roles.
> Protagonist (as wife):   You never trusted me either. You are a jealous husband.
> Director: Reverse roles.
> Protagonist: That is kinda true . . .

A Role Reversal Especially Helps an Individual Understand and Feel What it is Like to be Someone Else, to see the World from Someone Else's Point of View. This is poignantly illustrated in the following lines from Moreno.

> A meeting of two; eye to eye, face to face
> And when you are near I will tear your eyes out
> and place them instead of mine,
> and you will tear my eyes out
> and will place them instead of yours,
> then I will look at you with your eyes
> and you will look at me with mine.
>
> *Motto* (Moreno, 1946)

THE DRAMA.   There is, of course, no formula for the drama. It unfolds and may go into any direction according to the needs of the protagonist, the spontaneity of the participants, and the knowledge and imagination of the Director. Some psychodramatic scenes are moving and poignant; others may be plodding and boring. The movement and affect displayed by the participants are not always a measure of the benefit derived by the protagonist. A psychodrama may appear slow and uninteresting and still be a journey in exploration of one's feelings, thoughts, and attitudes.

The Sharing Phase.   Every human being goes through different experiences and every human life is unique. Feelings, however, are universal. When a protagonist goes through the drama of his or her life, no one in the audience has gone through precisely the same events. Almost everyone, however, can resonate to the protagonist's hurt, sadness, anger, and joy. No matter what the events depicted in the drama, feelings and memories are stimulated in the audience as well as the auxiliary egos. At the conclusion of the drama, the members of the group are asked to share these feelings and memories with each other and with the protagonist. Sharing is not interpreting; it is not giving advice. It is a sharing of one's self with others.

Psychodramatic Interventions

I stated above that a psychodramatic intervention can be brief, almost surgical in nature or that it may be a longer, more involved psychodrama. Both kinds of interventions will be illustrated below.

A BRIEF INTERVENTION.   There are no rules governing the choice of intervention. The Director will use his or her judgment and base the choice on the protagonist's needs, the prevailing circumstances, etc. My preference is to use a brief intervention when the conflict experienced by a group member inhibits communication within the group but is not, itself, the main focus of the interaction.

> This was Donna's last group session. She had, the time before, discussed the meaning and reason for terminating, and we all had agreed that she had indeed achieved her goals and that termination was indeed indicated. Donna was a very warm and nurturant person. She was very much liked by all the other group members, and everyone was affected by her leaving. The session started with some minutes of awkward silence. The silence was followed by somewhat meaningless and superficial interaction. At that time, I intervened as follows:

Director: I am feeling somewhat uncomfortable. We are talking about such trivial and superficial things and this is very unlike our group. I wonder if we are, perhaps, running away from something.

Paul (With tears in his eyes and a very sad expression):   I don't know what it is that we are running away from but I do know that I feel very, very sad at Donna's leaving.

Jane: I do, too. (Turning to Donna) Donna, it will be so lonely here without you. I know that I like everyone and everyone likes me, but you were the one that I always used to turn to for help.

At that moment the group gathered around Donna, and everyone seemed very depressed. Donna cried as various group members said their goodbyes. She then turned to Paul and Jane and said "I feel so bad about leaving you behind. I feel so worried about you. It's such a sad feeling to go. It's almost as if I really don't want to go, but I know I have . . . I have to. It's really very, very difficult. I don't feel right about it.

Director: Donna, would you write a letter to your two children? (Note: Donna has two teenage children, both of whom are in college.)

Donna (Surprised):   My children! What for?

Director: You'll see.

Donna: What shall I tell them?

Director: Whatever comes to your mind.

Donna: All right. Dear John and Dan, I am so proud of you. You are both such wonderful children. You have done so well for yourself. You are independent, self-reliant, and you have made me and your dad always very happy. I remember when I first went to work, how guilty I felt. We did not need the money, but I knew that I needed to do something about myself getting some independence, really find myself. I could not just stay home and be a housewife all my life. I knew you would do well without me, but I couldn't help but feel so guilty at the beginning and now I am so happy and so proud of you for what you've done.

Director (Interrupting):   Now, Donna, would you talk to Jane and Paul?

Donna (Turning to Jane and Paul):   That's true, you don't need me. You have your own strength. I know you will do well without me to support you. I feel alright now. I know it's OK to leave.

At that time, it seemed as if a pall of gloom had lifted from the group. The tension seemed released, and everyone wished Donna well and expressed both their sadness and joy at her departure.

Donna's transferential feelings toward Paul and Jane were not the group's main concern. The group's main concern was centered around Donna's departure. Nevertheless, Donna's feelings toward Paul and Jane were blocking the group's expression of feelings toward Donna's termination. As soon as Donna became aware of the transferential nature of her feelings, the blocking was removed and communication flowed more freely.

A MORE COMPLEX PSYCHODRAMA.   When the protagonist's conflict is the main concern of the group, it is my opionion that more involved action is called for. This will become apparent in the following illustration.

Participants: Dan (a Catholic priest in his late thirties), Ed, Tom, Tina, Liz, Jane, Mary, Rose.
The session started with some small talk and eventually focused on what members want out of life. Eventually, Dan stated that the only thing he ever wanted from life but never could get was a real meaningful relationship with another human being. There was so much poignancy in his voice that he immediately became the center of attention. In answer to the interested queries of the other group members, he shrugged stating that he really does not know why he cannot satisfy that simple yet so important need.

Director: Dan, I would like you, if you are agreeable and the group has no objections, to have a fantasy (Dan nods and the members of the group voice their approval). I would like you to imagine yourself with your eyes closed at the beginning of a very long field. At the other end of the field there is a not very distinguishable glow; that glow represents "the relationship." Between you and the glow are picket signs in the field. Each one of those picket signs represents an obstacle. Now concentrate on the picket signs and read what is on them.

Dan (concentrating hard):   I see three signs; I see fear written on one of them; hopelessness on the other one; and failure on the third one.

Director: I would like you to take three people in the group to play, if they are willing, the part of the obstacles.

Dan picks Tina to play Fear, Liz to play Hopelessness, and Jane to play Failure.

Director: Now, Dan, I would like you to look around and see if there is a person in the group to whom you were not able to relate even though you might have wanted to.

Dan points at Rose.

Director: Rose, you will be Dan's goal then, if it is okay with you. I would like you to stand at the other end of the room and just wait there. Dan will stay at this end of the room and Fear, Hopelessness, and Failure will sit down on the floor between you and Rose and I would like you, Dan, to have a dialogue with them. You may, if you wish, start with Fear.

Dan (to Fear):   Ever since I was a little boy, you stood in my way. I was never allowed to do anything. Don't do this, you'll get hurt. Don't do that, you'll get hurt. Didn't you realize that you always made me feel so frightened, so different.

Director: Now, reverse roles.

Dan (as Fear):   Don't blame me. I was only trying to protect you. You were the one who was always afraid to do things. You never wanted to take a chance. You always were a sissy, afraid to get hurt, afraid to get sick, afraid the little boys would beat you up, afraid to take chances. Jesus Christ, you make me sick.

Director: Now talk to Hopelessness.

Dan (to Hopelessness):   You have always been with me. Whatever I try to do, I never could do it with enthusiasm. I never felt that there was something I could look forward to. It was almost like a chronic state of despair inside me. What is the use? It will never happen. No matter how much I try, it never happens.

Director: Reverse roles.

Dan (as Hopelessness):   So, you never tried anything with the intent of finishing it up. Even before you tried something, deep down you were certain that there was no hope for you. Look at your brother, he was always full of enthusiasm. You make self-fulfilling prophecies occur.

Director: Now, talk to Failure.

Dan (to Failure):   Yeah, I know. What could I do? I made you happen. You have been with me all of the time. How can I be successful at anything when I am afraid to do things, when I am afraid to start things and when I have no hope. It is almost like I have been programmed to make you happen.

Director: Reverse roles.

Dan (as Failure): That's right, that's right. You make me happen and I am your constant companion. You have me for as long as you live. I will always be with you.

Director: Now, you all have an idea of who you are and what you have to say. Dan, your task would be to go past them, to overwhelm them, to defeat them. Now, your task, Fear, Hopelessness, and Failure, will be to resist him and not let him go past you. Okay? Start the action.

Fear: Well, come on. Do something. You have never had the courage to start anything. Always frightened, always scared. Don't take chances; don't try to do things. Don't always stay locked up within yourself. Come out and do it. What do you expect? Someone to be behind you all the time and push you?

Hopelessness: Don't even try. Don't even try. You know you are not going to make it. There really is no hope for you. No hope for anything you have ever done or will ever do in your life.

Failure: That's what I mean! You are and you will always be a complete failure. Look at your peers. Look at the people around you. Look at all the things they have achieved. Oh, but not you. You will always be an utter, complete failure. I am literally ashamed of you.

During this time Dan remains silent and does not say a word.

Director: What's the matter, Dan? It looks like they are getting the best of you. Do you need any help? You'll never get anywhere unless you fight them back.

Dan (with tears in his eyes and a voice choked with emotion): Damn, you all sound like my father. That's what he would always say. He never, never gave me any encouragement. Never gave me any hope. Always, he predicted that I would fail and Goddamn that's what always happened. I always fail. I am just sick of it all. (he cries.)

Director: Dan, I would like you to pick someone from the group who could play the part of your father, if he is willing.

Dan: I think Ed could. He kind of looks like him.

Director: Okay, I would like Fear, Hopelessness, and Failure to move away for a while and I would like you, Dan, to face your father and have it out with him. I would also like to ask you if you need a double.

Dan: Yes. I think I could use one. I am not up to facing my Dad all by myself. I would like Tom to be my Double. (The therapist arranges a scene in Dan's home. He and his father are supposedly in their living room and Dan's task is to talk to his father and make him aware of what he has done to him as he was growing up.) There is a five-minute silence. Dan swallows, squirms and says nothing.

Double: It's tough to face my father. I don't know how to start this.

Dan: Yes, it is tough. I have never done that before.

Double: I have never faced my father before, and it is hard to do it, but I would really like to.

Dan: That's true, Dad. I would like to face you at last and tell you some of the things that I have been meaning to tell you for many years.

Father: What are you talking about?

Dan: You know, as I was growing up, you never instilled any confidence in me. You never made me fell like I was capable of doing things.

Father: What are you talking about? Dan, you know I tried to be a good father to you. I protected you. But I couldn't make you into something you are not. You have always been a weak, sniveling failure.

Double: There he goes! doing it to me again.

Dan: That's right. There you go doing it to me again.

Father: Doing what to you?

Dan: Making me feel like I'm shit.

Father: That's no way to talk to me. That's no way to talk to your father. Especially at your age and being a priest and all.

Dan: That's got nothing to do with it.

Father: That's got everything to do with it. You don't behave properly. You never behave properly, and of course you failed at everything you did.

Dan: (silence).

Director: Dan, I would like you to change the format a little bit. I am going to give you a specific task to do and this task is to tell your father that he will never succeed in making you feel as inadequate and as hopeless as he has in the past. Now you, Dad, you will make it very difficult for Dan to tell you that. Whatever he says, wait until he begins to develop his thought and interrupt him. Don't worry about being rational or logical. Whatever he says, just say the opposite and keep interrupting him. Don't give him a chance to develop his thought. As for you, Dan, I will give you a way of going around him. Everytime you want your father to listen to you, you will raise your hand and say "shut up." As you say that, you will have five seconds to say what you want to say. After five seconds I will motion to your father with my finger to start talking again. But, you can keep shutting him up all of the time. You don't have to let him interrupt you. Everytime he opens his mouth you can shut him up with your voice and your hand, Is that clear, Dan?

Dan: Okay.

Director: Alright, let's have some action.

Dan: Okay, Dad! It's about time I tell you what I meant to tell you for such a long time.

Father (interrupting): Tell me what. I have been here waiting for you to say something and you are not saying anything. Well, come on.

Dan: Well, you don't give me a chance.

Father (interrupting): I have been shutting up, trying for you to tell me something.

Dan (interrupting): Shut up. All my life you have made me feel like a nothing. You never gave me any encouragement. You never tried to make me feel that I was capable of doing things.

Father (interrupting): That's not true. I always encouraged you. I always told you how good you were at everything.

Dan: Shut up and listen to me. But, that is enough. You are never going to do it again.

Father: (trying to interrupt).

Dan (screaming at the top of his lungs): Shut up. But never, never again are you going to make me feel that way. It is enough! I have had enough and I am not going to listen to you anymore.

Father (interrupting): That's no way to talk . . .

Dan (screaming): SHUT UP! SHUT UP! SHUT UP! (continues to scream on top of his voice in a very angry tone) Never again am I going to allow you to belittle me and steal my self-confidence away from me. You hear me. Never again, I am sick of you. I am sick of everything you have done to me. It is about time I became my own man.

Director: (motions to father not to interrupt).

Dan (continues in a very loud voice): And, now I want you to leave here. Just go. Get the hell out of here. I don't ever want to see you again.

Father leaves the room. Dan is very agitated. He paces up and down, breathing very heavily, clenching his fists. Slowly he begins to relax.

Director: You know, Dan, every coin has two sides. There is night and there is day; there is warm and there is cold and so far you have only faced one side of your Fear, Hopelessness, and Failure. The other side is Courage, Hope, and Success, and I would like you to meet them now.

Director: (motions to Fear, Hopelessness, and Failure). Now you will be on the other side of that same coin.

Fear (comes close to Dan who is sitting on the floor): I want to tell you, I was so impressed by the way you faced your father down. My God, Dan, you were not afraid. There was so much courage in you. I really felt like I was your courage. Like I was with you when you were going through this ordeal. It was just wonderful and I'd like to stay with you. (Tina holds Dan's hand. Dan reaches for her and hugs her and says "I would like you to be next to me").

Hopelessness (She in turn comes close to Dan, faces him): There was hope in what you said, Dan. I can't believe that a man like you, with your sensitivity and the strength and the guts which you have just shown, can go through life alone. That just can't be. I would like so much to give you what I am feeling now, which is so much hope for you, for your future, for your happiness. I really like you. (She leans over, hugs Dan, and sits by his side.)

Failure (She faces Dan): There isn't much for me to say, Dan, after what Tina and Liz have said. I thing your failures were all made by yourself. You will never again fail if you keep with you the hope that you are feeling now and the courage that you have shown. (She hugs Dan and also sits next to him.)

Dan holds the three women's hands and his eyes are misty.

Director: Dan is there anything else that you would like to do?

Dan (forcefully stands up): Yes, there is. (He goes to Rose at the other end of the room.) Rose, you have been in the group for seven months. From the first time I saw you I liked you a lot. You are a little bit like me. You are shy, not very forward, and I felt a kinship for you and I never dared tell you, but I do now. Somehow I am not afraid any more. I would like you to be my friend. To really be a good friend.

Rose (laughs): You know, Dan, I have felt that way since the first time I came into the group also. I think I felt your fear. I felt your shyness and your timidity, and I liked you like a brother. But it was kind of strange. You are a Catholic priest and I am Jewish and a woman and I did not want to be misunderstood, but I'd be honored and and happy to be your friend.

Dan takes her by the hand over to the cluster formed by the other three women. Then Dan moves over to his father and says "I don't want you to be old and alone and without friends. I want you to be with us, but damn it, one word out of you, one single word out of the past and out you go again. But, come in now."

At the conclusion of the above drama, participants did a lot of sharing, reminiscing, and talking about their own childhood, their own experiences, and their relationships with their parents.

The above psychodrama holds a very special meaning for me. At that time, I was training a group of mental health professionals. As part of the ongoing training and in order to promote the use of psychodrama we had decided to role-play a psychodrama for the benefit of a professional audience at the Community Mental Health Center of St. Francis General Hospital, Pittsburgh, Pennsylvania. The group of clients who had gone through the drama described above gave to the group in training permission to reenact that experience. The only condition for granting their permission was that they would be allowed to be in the audience incognito. The group in training did such a magnificent job of reproducing the drama and the people to whom the experience had happened were so moved, that they spontaneously identified themselves, walked on the stage, and congratulated the actors.

I will end this section by explaining the reasons for using, on rare occasions, a more classical approach, that is, beginning with a warm-up, choosing a protagonist, etc. There are times, admittedly few, when group members are not aware of any pressing matters. The silence and lack of interaction are not used to avoid. There is a certain laziness, a certain contentment in the air exemplified, perhaps, by the following comment of a group member "I feel mellow, don't ever want to budge. Why don't you do something, Doc?" Things would eventually happen even if the therapist takes no initiative. On rare occasions, however, I take the initiative, and this is perceived by the group members as a change of pace for which they are appreciative.

It does not take very long for people who feel safe and trust each other to learn to communicate, to be in touch with and share their feelings about each other as such feelings occur. Communication within the group flows freely, and group members become very important to each other. As stated earlier, however, their lives unfold outside the group. The group is often used to solve problems and conflicts that have occurred elsewhere and at other times. Very often, these conflicts and problems are solved through a group interaction. There are times, however, when the group can do no more than show support, acceptance, and understanding. The conflicts still remain. At such times, the therapist may intervene. The nature of the therapist's intervention depends on the therapist's orientation, training, and preferences. I use psychodrama; analytically oriented therapists, Gestalt therapists, behavior therapists, and so on use different approaches. In addition to the merits of pshchodrama mentioned earlier in this addendum, I favor the use of psychodrama because it involves more than one person; especially when the group is not large, everyone has a chance to participate, to vicariously share in another person's experience and to derive the feeling of having been helpful and important. When the drama is completed, the conflict solved or alleviated, the group takes over again and my role once more reverts to that of a facilitator of a desirable process.

The use of psychodrama is a difficult and complex undertaking. The same way as the acquisition of techniques without a solid generic training is to be discouraged, an adequate background in a mental health field with only a smattering of techniques is insufficient to become a good psychodramatist. The training is involved, time-consuming, and cannot be acquired only through readings. The purpose of this addendum, in addition to illustrating the uses of some psychodramatic techniques, is to encourage and stimulate the reader to seek the necessary training.

SUMMARY

I. Psychodrama: A theory or a set of techniques

While built upon complex theoretical underpinnings, psychodrama can be looked at as a set of techniques of such elegance and flexibility that it can be used within any kind of theoretical framework.

II. Glossary and techniques

    1. A Psychodrama

    A. The Warm-up

    B. The Protagonist

    C. The soliloquy

    D. Auxiliary egos

    E. The double

        a) Doubling as a client-centered reflection of feelings

        b) Doubling as a matching of words, feelings and tone of voice

        c) Doubling as incomplete sentences

    F. Role reversal

        a) A role reversal helps the auxiliary ego become acquainted with his or her role.

        b) A role reversal helps an individual reincorporate one's projections

        c) A role reversal helps an individual understand and feel what it is like to be someone else.

    G. The drama

    H. The sharing phase

    2. Psychodramatic interventions

    A. A brief intervention

    B. A more complex psychodrama

SUGGESTED READINGS IN PSYCHODRAMA

Blatner, H. *Acting-in: Practical aspects of psychodramatic methods.* New York: Springer, 1973.

Corsini, R. J. The "behind the back" technique in psychodrama. *Group Psychotherapy,* 1953, *6,* 102–109.

Enneis, J. M. A note on the organization of the St. Elizabeth Hospital psychodrama program. *Group Psychotherapy,* 1950, *3,* 253–255.

Enneis, J. M. The dynamics of group and action processes in therapy: An analysis of the warm-up in psychodrama. *Group Psychotherapy,* 1951, *4,* 17–22.

Fine, L. J. Nonverbal aspects of psychodrama. In J. Masserman, J. L. Moreno (Eds.). *Progress in psychotherapy.* New York: Grune & Stratton, 1959.

Hollander, C. The mirror technique as a psychodramatic encounter. *Group Psychotherapy,* 1967, *20,* 25–31.

Lippitt, R. The auxiliary chair technique. *Group Psychotherapy,* 1958, *11,* 823.

Moreno, J. L. *Psychodrama, Vol. I.* New York: Beacon House, 1946; Third Edition, 1970.

Moreno, J. L. *Psychodrama, Vol. II.* New York: Beacon House, 1946; Third Edition, 1970.

Moreno, J. L. *Psychodrama, Vol. III.* New York: Beacon House, 1946; Third Edition, 1970.

Moreno, J. L. The theater of spontaneity: an introduction to psychodrama. In *Psychodrama monograph 22.* New York: Beacon House, 1947.

Moreno, J. L., *Who shall survive? 2nd Edition.* New York: Beacon House, 1953.

Moreno, J. L. Psychodrama. In S. Arieti (Ed.), *American handbook of psychiatry, Vol. 2.* New York: Basic Books, 1959.

Moreno, J. L. Therapeutic vehicles and the concept of surplus reality. *Group Psychotherapy,* 1965, *18,* 211–216.

Moreno, J. L. The triadic system: Psychodrama-sociometry-group psychotherapy. *Group Psychotherapy,* 1970, *23,* 16.

Moreno, Z. T. Psychodramatic techniques. *Acta Psychotherapeutica Psychosomatica et Orthopedagogica,* 1959, *7,* 197–206.

Moreno, Z. T. A survey of psychodramatic techniques. *Group Psychotherapy,* 1959, *12,* 5–14.

Moreno, Z. T. Psychodramatic rules, techniques and adjunctive methods. *Group Psychotherapy,* 1965, *18,* 73–86.

Naar, R. Termination. *Group Psychotherapy and Psychodrama,* 1974, *27,* (1–4) 55–58.

Naar, R. A psychodramatic intervention with a T. A. framework in individual and group psychotherapy. *Group Psychotherapy, Psychodrama and Sociometry,* 1977, *30,* 127–134.

Sacks, J. M. The judgment technique in psychodrama. *Group Psychotherapy,* 1965, *18,* 69–72.

Sacks, J. M. Psychodrama, the warm-up. *Group Psychotherapy,* 1967, *20,* 118.

Sacks, J. M. The letter. *Group Psychotherapy and Psychodrama,* 1974, *27,* (1–4) 184–190.

Sacks, J. M. The psychodrama group: formation and beginnings. *Group Process,* 1976, 7, 59–78

Weiner, H. B., & Sachs, J. M. Warm up and sum up. *Group Psychotherapy,* 1969, *22,* 84–102.

IN RETROSPECT

This book is now finished. The undertaking was hard, but very exciting. I have learned much through writing these pages. I was able to clarify for myself, and hopefully for others, concepts that were vague. I understand better what I am doing as a group therapist. By distancing myself from and by writing about my behavior in group, I became aware of much about myself and realized many of my mistakes. I believe that through this writing, I have become a better group therapist.

Writing this book has done even more for me. It has enabled me to relive some memorable experiences in my life. I recaptured moments of joy, of love, of sadness, despair, and triumph. It has helped me recognize, once more, with admiration and respect the power and strength generated by a group of people open to each other, a strength that brought back from the abyss Daniel the priest and Nancy who wanted to die after being told that she would lose both breasts.

Writing *A Primer of Group Psychotherapy* has helped me get in touch with my feelings toward the people whose lives I have shared. I searched and I believe that I found the words that describe my feelings and it is with these words that I will end my book.

To The Group

You and I
Have looked into each other
And accepted what we saw.

You and I were not afraid.

You and I
Have cried together
Shared our weakness and our strength.

You and I have known each other well.

You and I
Have learned together
In so many wonderful ways.

You and I have grown together.

I think, perhaps,
You and I
Have loved each other.

Pittsburgh, Pennsylvania
New Year's Eve, 1979

REFERENCES

American Group Psychotherapy Association. *Guidelines for the training of group psychotherapists.* New York: American Group Psychotherapy Association, 1978.

American Psychological Association. *Ethical standards of psychologists,* 1979 Revision. Washington, D.C.: American Psychological Association, 1979.

Bernardez, T., & Stein, T. S. Separating the sexes in group therapy: An experiment with men's and women's groups. *International Journal of Group Psychotherapy,* 1979, *29, 4,* 493–502.

Berne, E. *Games people play.* New York: Grove Press, 1964.

Bion, W. R. *Experiences in groups.* New York: Basic Books, 1959. Cited by Rioch, M. J. The work of Wilfred Bion on groups. In C. J. Sager & H. S. Kaplan (Eds.). *Progress in groups and family therapy.* New York: Brunner/Mazel, 1972, pp. 18–32.

Birk, L., & Brinkley-Birk, A. W., Psychoanalysis and behavior therapy. *American Journal of Psychiatry,* 1974, *137, 5,* 499–510.

Cox, M. Group psychotherapy as a redefining process. *International Journal of Group Psychotherapy,* 1973, *23, 4,* 465–473.

Dollard, J., & Miller, N. E. *Personality and psychotherapy.* New York: McGraw-Hill, 1950.

Durkin, H. E. Analytical group therapy and general systems theory. In C. J. Sager & H. S. Kaplan, (Eds.), *Progress in group and family therapy.* New York: Brunner/Mazel, 1972, pp. 9–17.

Forer, Bertram R. The taboo against touching in psychotherapy. *Psychotherapy: Theory, Research and Practice,* 1969, *6, 4,* 229–231.

Fowler, H. *Curiosity and exploratory behavior.* New York: Macmillan, 1965.

Freud, A. *The ego and the mechanisms of defense.* New York: International Universities Press, 1954.

Freud, S. *The basic writings of Sigmund Freud.* New York: Random House, 1938.

Greer, Valerie J., & Sacks, J. M., *Bibliography of Psychodrama.* Unpublished manuscript, 1973.

Hall, C. S., & Lindzey, G. *Theories of personality.* New York: John Wiley, 1957.

Holroyd, J. C., & Brodsky, A. M. Psychologists' attitudes and practices regarding erotic and nonerotic physical contact with patients. *American Psychologist,* 1977, *10,* 843–849.

Horowitz, L. A group-centered approach to group psychotherapy. *International Journal of Group Psychotherapy,* 1977, *27, 4,* 423–439.

Howard, J. *Please touch: A guided tour of the human potential movement.* New York: McGraw-Hill, 1970.

Kagan, N. Issues in encounter. *The Counseling Psychologist,* 1970, *2.2,* 34–38.

Koch, S. An implicit image of man. In N. Solomon & B. Berzon (Eds.). *New perspectives on encounter groups.* San Francisco: Jossey-Bass, 1972, pp. 30–52.

Laking, M. Response to Coulson. *The counseling psychologist,* 1970, *2.2,* 34–38.

Mintz, E. E. On the rationale of touch in psychotherapy. In C. J. Sager & H. S. Kaplan (Eds.). *Progress in group and family therapy.* New York: Brunner/Mazel, 1972.

Moreno, J. L. *The words of the father.* New York: Beacon House, 1941.

Moreno, J. L. *Psychodrama, Vol. I.* Revised ed. New York: Beacon House, 1964.

Naar, R. Client-centered and behavior therapies: Their peaceful coexistence: a case study. *Journal of Abnormal Psychology,* 1970, *76 (2),* 155–160.

Naar, R. What, when and for what: A suggested multi/modal approach to therapy. *Psychotherapy: Theory, Research and Practice,* 1979, *16 (1),* 9–17.

Patterson, C. H. Relationship theory and/or behavior therapy? *Psychotherapy: Theory, Research and Practice,* 1968, *5,* 226–233.

Perls, F. *The gestalt approach and eye witness to therapy.* New York: Science and Behavior Books, 1973.

Polster, E., & Polster, M. *Gestalt therapy integrated.* New York: Brunner/ Mazel, 1973.

Rogers, C. R. *Client-centered therapy.* Boston: Houghton-Mifflin, 1951.

Rogers, C. R. *On becoming a person.* Boston: Houghton-Mifflin, 1961.

Sacks, J. M. The reformed auxiliary ego technique: A psychodramatic rekindling of hope. *Group Psychotherapy,* 1970, *23,* 118–126.

Sacks, J. M. The "shut-up" technique for releasing inhibited anger. *Group Psychotherapy, Psychodrama and Sociometry,* 1976, *29,* 52–62.

Sager, C. J., & Kaplan, H. S. (Eds.). *Progress in group and family therapy.* New York: Brunner/Mazel, 1972.

Shaffer, J. B. P. & Galinsky, D. M. *Models of group therapy and sensitivity training.* Englewood Cliffs, N.J., Prentice-Hall, 1974.

Siroka, R. The death scene in psychodrama. *Group Psychotherapy,* 1968, *21,* 202–205.

Slavson, S. R. *Analytic group psychotherapy.* New York: Columbia University Press, 1950.

Szasz, T. S. *The myth of mental illness.* New York: Harper & Row, 1961.

Truax, C. B., & Carkhuff, R. R. *Toward effective counseling and psychotherapy.* Chicago, Aldine, 1967.

Villon, F. *Oeuvres.* Paris: Gilbert Jeune, 1952.

Wise, T. Utilization of group process in training oncology fellows. *International Journal of Group Psychotherapy,* 1977, *27,* 105–111.

Yalom, I. D. *The theory and practice of group psychotherapy.* New York: Basic Books, 1978.

Zimet, C. Developmental task and crisis groups: The application of group therapy to maturational processes. *Psychotherapy: Theory, Research and Practice,* 1979, *16, 1,* 208.

INDEX